Enjoy cooking!

OLIVE OIL, SEA SALT & PEPPER

OLIVE OIL, SEA SALT & PEPPER

healing with fresh foods

JENN CROVATO

Photography by RENÉE COMET

HILTON PUBLISHING

Hilton Publishing Company
Chicago, IL

Direct all correspondence to:
Hilton Publishing Company
1630 45th St. Suite B101
Munster, IN 46321
219–922–4868

www.hiltonpub.com

ISBN 978-0-9716067-7-7

Library of Congress Cataloging-in-Publication Data

Olive oil, sea salt & pepper.
    pages cm
ISBN 978-0-9716067-7-7
1. Sautéing. I. Title: Olive oil, sea salt, and pepper.
TX689.4.O45 2012
641.7'7—dc23
                    2012042358

Design: KATE MCCONNELL
Photography Assistant: STEVEN REDFEARN
Prop Styling: AUDREY WEPPLER
Food Styling: JENN CROVATO
Copy Editor: BETH MCCONNELL
Production: OMNISTUDIO

Author photo location: Restaurant ROUGE 24
Printed in Canada

In Memory of Joseph E. Robert, Jr.

"In the inspirational spirit of Joe, I would like to
make a difference in the lives of others
by presenting cooking in an uncomplicated form
that will motivate people to get back into the kitchen
and eat fresh, healthy food."

— Jenn

TO MY FAMILY,

who have unconditionally loved and supported me
through all of my good and not so good decisions,
guided me along the way and always been my biggest cheerleaders,
Thank you!

TO COLE AND CHEYENNE,

for all of the nights, weekends and holidays I spent working,
thank you for your tolerance and understanding. I love you both!

TO HILTON,

thank you for always believing in me
and helping me through the process of bringing this dream to print.

Thank you to all of my friends for their relentless encouragement.

A WORD FROM THE DOCTOR

In America, eating good tasting food is, undeniably, one of life's most treasured pleasures. For most of us who work hard all day, enjoying a meal with colleagues, friends and family may actually be the best part of the day and the only time we feel connected, protected, relaxed, loved and at ease. During times of pure joy and celebration, or during times of grief and sadness, eating delicious food has importance in our lives. Food satisfies and nurtures us, but eating the wrong food, or too much of it, can do quite the opposite. After 18 years as a heart and lung surgeon, it's overwhelmingly sad for me to see people who, due to sickness, poor lifestyle choices and poor eating habits, lose the fight for life. It is disheartening to me to know that different personal choices could have extended and saved many of those lives. Americans, for the most part, can live longer and healthier. But it takes knowledge, empowerment and a little courage to make smart diet, exercise, stress reduction and other lifestyle choices.

Let's look at some scary but true health facts:

* Heart disease, strokes, diabetes and cancers account for 90% of deaths and chronic illnesses in America today.
* Well over 50% of Americans are obese or overweight.
* Obesity and being overweight are directly or indirectly responsible for heart disease, diabetes and strokes.
* Obesity is an independent risk factor for heart failure; simply stated, being obese can cause heart failure.
* America's healthcare costs are among the highest of any developed nation in the world and, in part, this is due to Americans' lifestyle choices.
* Americans who know more, who embrace wellness and who eat healthier live longer than those who do not. It's as simple as that.
* Patients who are committed to eating healthy foods and to healthy lifestyle choices will recover more quickly from illness then those who are not.

Though these facts are scary and perhaps downright depressing, don't be discouraged. We have the knowledge and tools we need to live longer and healthier. As Americans, we need to simply make the commitment to do so. Now, for some of us it's not going to be easy but it can be done with an unbending focus on wellness, a commitment to eating the right foods and, lastly, the right road map and tools to keep us on track.

OLIVE OIL, SEA SALT, & PEPPER is an incredible and revolutionary tool that is empowering and life changing. From the health benefits of the three basic ingredients, to the focus on fresh, unprocessed foods, to the methods of cooking, OLIVE OIL, SEA SALT & PEPPER provides a proven and easy-to-follow road map to longevity and a quality life. Embrace its concepts and you will experience improved health and wellness.

I enthusiastically endorse OLIVE OIL, SEA SALT & PEPPER. It's excellent and a must have for those who cherish some of life's most treasured gifts: really good food and good health.

Hilton M Hudson II, MD, FACS, FCCP
Cardiac-Thoracic Surgeon
CEO, HPC, Inc.
Chicago, IL, USA

CONTENTS

I COOK. IT'S WHO I AM and how I function.
It is how I relate and how I nurture. Cooking comes
as naturally to me as breathing and I use it daily to
entertain, to nourish, to heal and to celebrate. As instinc-
tive as cooking is for me, I understand it produces
dread, uncertainty, fear and downright discouragement
for many people.

Olive Oil, Sea Salt & Pepper is for those who want to
serve great tasting, healthy meals every time without
wasting endless hours flipping through cookbooks and
searching online only to find complicated recipes with
many obscure or expensive ingredients. This is a col-
lection of straightforward recipes that emphasize fresh,
quality ingredients and careful, but easy-to-master
preparation. With *Olive Oil, Sea Salt & Pepper* as your
staples you will always have on hand what you need to
create healthy, flavorful meals.

Olive Oil, Sea Salt & Pepper is for those who walk
through the farmer's markets, admire the produce and
yearn to know what to do with it. Now you can choose
the freshest local and seasonal produce, take it home and
create truly delicious meals. As the seasons change, so
does the bounty. This book will encourage you to take
advantage of the best of each season and to try new or
less-familiar ingredients by giving you the simple steps
to turn everything from rutabagas to Brussels sprouts
into nourishing creations and healthy meals.

WHY THIS BOOK AT THIS TIME?

THE CONCEPT OF *Olive Oil, Sea Salt & Pepper* came to me after years of hearing the same questions and comments again and again: "How do you do that?" or "You must have done something more than that!" or "I could never get it to taste so good!" It also emerged as I observed my clients develop an appreciation for the pure, clean taste of real food. I watched their palates mature as they made the switch from prepared food to fresh food, from globally supplied produce to fresh local produce, from corn fed to grass fed, from genetically altered to organic. I saw them turn from heavy sauces on their vegetables to blanched vegetables and from deep fried to oven roasted. What happened is that they discovered the true taste of real food. No longer were they *trying* to eat healthy. They simply were eating healthy because that's what they craved. They finally knew what it was to be nourished.

This book is intended for every skill level and every dietary regimen. It is for the novice who feels uneasy in the kitchen and the hurried mom who wants quick, non-processed, tasty meals for finicky and allergic 3-foot-tall food critics. Moreover, it is for the competent cook who seeks new food combinations and easier methods that still meet a discriminating palate, as well as the person who desperately *wants* to eat healthier but believes it will require more time and effort than she or he has to spare.

I have a deep desire to call everyone back into the kitchen. It's where life happens, generations connect, stories are communicated, problems are solved and work is shared. It's where the phone is put aside and texts are ignored so people can simply talk. My hope is that when you learn how straightforward and effortless these methods are you will prefer roasting some veggies and sautéing a piece of fish to eating out because it is actually *easier* and it *tastes better*. Plus, with three basic ingredients for each recipe, you'll always have what you need right in your pantry.

HEALING WITH FRESH FOODS

HEALTH

Why is it so important to learn to cook fresh food? Because it empowers us! Today, America has the unique distinction of being classified as the least healthy country in the developed world. Two-thirds of Americans are statistically overweight and heart disease is the number one cause of death. In many cases, heart disease, stroke, diabetes, obesity and some cancers are diet related illnesses directly linked to the food choices we make. Yet most people still choose to take the risk. Choosing to eat fresh, natural food rather than processed food is like choosing not to smoke. When you choose to smoke, you have to know that, in the long term, you are putting yourself at risk for lung cancer. Processed foods, over the long term, put you at risk for heart disease, obesity, diabetes and possibly cancer.

The painful reality is that, without change, this generation of Americans won't live as long as their parents. Now is the time to turn things around. And it can be done because diet-related diseases are preventable. We each have the power to improve our own health and to influence the health of those we love by making better choices about the food we eat and prepare for our friends and family.

THE SIGNIFICANCE OF EATING LOCAL

If you want to make excellent food, you need to start with excellent ingredients.

I remember fondly my first trip to Italy as a teenager. That's where I discovered the goodness of the food. I watched as Signora prepared dinner and was determined to remake the meals once I returned home. I tried many times to recreate her dishes but none of them turned out as well.

At age 20, I spent a year cooking in different regions of Italy. It was there that I picked up on the key to Italian cooking. Each dish was composed of ingredients that were local and in season and that's why they tasted so much better! For the best results, use ingredients that are at their seasonal peak and master the simplicity of preparation.

To find sources of local, seasonal products, look online at Local Harvest: http://www.localharvest.org/. This web site has a wealth of information and it is very helpful for locating local farmer's markets and community-supported agriculture.

HOW MUCH?

The amount of ingredients used in a recipe seems to put people on the edge. Everyone always asks, "How much? I need an EXACT, precise amount!"

No you do not. Relax.

Do as much or as little as suits you. Remember, measurements can be adjusted based on what is in your refrigerator, what is available at the store, what you like or don't like or the number of people for whom you are cooking. It is always okay to buy a little more, make a little more and keep the leftovers in the refrigerator. Enjoy them for lunch the next day or take the next night off from cooking. But while precision isn't necessary, or even desirable, some guidelines will help:

Q. HOW MUCH FISH OR MEAT DO I BUY?

A. I calculate 6 – 8 ounces per person for a seated dinner, and 4 – 6 ounces per person for a buffet. If you are trying to lower your cholesterol or keep your weight down, limit your portion size to 2 – 4 ounces and bulk up on your vegetables.

Q. HOW MUCH OLIVE OIL?

A. Start with about 1 – 2 tablespoons. You can always add more if needed. Remember, you can always add to, but you can't take away. Make sure there is enough in the pan or on the vegetables to coat them. If the pan or vegetables look dry, just add a little more.

Q. HOW MUCH SEA SALT AND PEPPER ON VEGETABLES?

A. Until it tastes good. Add, taste, add, taste. This will make you a cook! But season a little at a time. It's also very important to season in layers. Make sure every component in the dish is seasoned. It's tough to develop the flavor of each component when you add your sea salt and pepper at the end.

Here's an example: You are sautéing onions, mushrooms and spinach. You start by sautéing onions, season them, then you add mushrooms, season again, then spinach and season again. By adding a little at a time you will have a more flavorful end product.

Q. HOW MUCH SEA SALT AND PEPPER ON MEAT OR FISH?

A. Make sure sea salt and pepper are covering both sides of the meat or fish you are cooking. Thicker cuts like NY Strip, beef tenderloin and tuna steak can take lots of sea salt & pepper. Thinner cuts like tilapia require less.

ABOUT ME

Throughout my life I have been blessed with support and encouragement. For this I am so grateful. The combination of those people who believed in me and those who did not drove me and made me who I am today.

From the age of five I was encouraged to be in the kitchen. We made homemade pasta, we made potato gnocchi and we always made our own pizza dough. I felt pretty comfortable with food preparation early on and cooking became my source of self-expression. By age eight I was expected to make dinner twice a week and regularly alternated between chicken breast Milanese and pasta shells with ricotta, bacon and peas. At age 10, I was catering birthday parties with homemade pizzas and cakes. At age 13, I was selling "pepperoni rolls" to teachers and delivering pizzas to neighbors by skateboard. I saved up enough money to go to Italy that summer, staying in Torino for a time with our dear friends the Chiavazzas and vacationing with their family off the coast of Rome for the month of August. This was the first time I was exposed to authentic Italian cuisine and I was intrigued by its simplicity.

At age 17, when I announced my plans to become a stunt woman, my mom suggested I might consider a culinary career. Although it was hard to take that jump from the movie set to the kitchen, cooking was something I always enjoyed. So, with hesitation, I agreed to visit the Culinary Institute of America in Hyde Park, New York. A short walk through the kitchen corridors had me hooked and I immediately began working on the requirements for application and admission. Attending the CIA as an 18 year old was both intimidating and highly motivating. I knew I belonged there and was up to the challenge.

Throughout externship and after graduation I was mentored by and worked with Roberto Donna at his trattoria *I Matti* and his flagship restaurant *Galileo* in Washington, D.C. Roberto was supportive of my decision to spend one year in Italy and he paved the way for me to do just that. In 1997 I moved from the south of Italy to the north and back down again…cooking my way through the country…from a small kitchen in Santa Dominica, Calabria…to illustrious establishments in both Portofino and Imola, with Chef Valentino Mercatili,…to various restaurants in Piedmonte, Liguria, Lievi, Salerno, Agropoli and Ana Capri. This was the most influential experience of my career.

After returning home and another stint at *Galileo*, motherhood led me to work as an on-site chef for an exclusive Washington, D.C., caterer. That experience exposed me to the world of entertaining and events. I was cooking regularly for high-profile, high-powered business and political clients. With six years behind me, the combination of restaurant and catering experience led me to work as a private chef for Joseph E. Robert Jr.

Working in this capacity required the flexibility to plan a soccer party for a six-year-old that often was followed by a dinner for a crown prince. In an average week, I was preparing lunches for Hollywood entertainers and dinners for politicians and other influential people in both Washington, D.C., and Beaver Creek, Colorado, where my employer had a second home.

Joe was a friend as well as my boss. A self-made man, he taught me to dream big and to work relentlessly for whatever I want in life. Joe was diagnosed with brain cancer in February of 2009. It was when Joe became ill that I began writing this book. Even though I was still cooking for Joe, my job changed. The big parties, business dinners and power entertaining all stopped. To fill my time, I wrote. It was tough to watch this larger-than-life man who had worked so hard for everything he had lose it all due to his health. Joe fought his illness for close to three years and lost his battle on December 7, 2011. Thank you Joe, not only for everything you did for me, but for the thousands of children who benefited and continue to benefit from your generosity. You have been and will always be deeply missed by all you have touched. In the inspirational spirit of Joe, I would like to make a difference in the lives of others by presenting cooking in an uncomplicated form that will motivate people to get back into the kitchen and eat fresh, healthy food.

Jenn Crovato, left, along with sister Christi and mother Terri, peeling tomatoes for canning in 1982.

HEALTH BENEFITS: OLIVE OIL

SEA SALT

PEPPER

GARLIC

OLIVE OIL

TYPES

Olive oil is made by pressing or crushing olives and its varieties depend on the degree to which it is processed. Olive oil is the only vegetable oil that can be consumed as it is, freshly pressed from the fruit.

Here is the lowdown on olive oil:

EXTRA LIGHT

Extra light olive oil undergoes considerable processing and only retains a very mild olive flavor. "Light" olive oil is a marketing concept and not a classification of olive oil grades. The term might make you think it contains less fat or is better for you but it is completely unregulated and, therefore, there is no real standard for its contents. Light olive oil is sometimes mixed with other vegetable oils.

REGULAR OR PURE

Regular or pure olive oil has been chemically refined and filtered to neutralize both undesirable strong tastes and acid content. This olive oil is of lower quality and usually the least expensive. "Pure" olive oil is made by adding a little extra virgin olive oil to refined olive oil. It is a lesser grade oil that is also labeled as simply "olive oil" in the U.S.

VIRGIN

Olive oil labeled virgin means the olive oil was produced without any chemical additives so it contains no refined oil and comes from the second pressing. Virgin refers to the fact that the olive oil has been less handled or manipulated during processing.

EXTRA VIRGIN

Extra virgin olive oil comes from the first press only and is the highest quality olive oil with perfect flavor, aroma and balanced acidity. This olive oil is less processed than virgin olive oil and has a very delicate flavor.

COLD PRESSED

Cold pressed olive oil is another unregulated label description. Back when olive oil was pressed the second time using hot water and steam to extract the last drop, the heat during the second pressing took away the delicate flavors. Today, premium olive oil is cold pressed, which means the olives are gently warmed to room temperature to avoid loss of taste and pressing is done in winter, when it is cold, to further retain the flavor.

Here is what you need to know:
You only need two types of olive oil: one to cook with and one to finish (or drizzle) with. Using cold pressed olive oil is not recommended for cooking because the high heat destroys its beneficial qualities. Labels that read "Olive Oil" are great for high heat cooking, such as sautéing. Less expensive extra virgin olive oil is also fine to cook with. Save the expensive cold pressed extra virgin olive oil to "finish" dishes. Drizzle this olive oil on top of salads, pastas, grilled vegetables, fish and meats after they are cooked. Stay away from the labels that read "Light" or "Extra Light" olive oil. The less the olive oil is handled, the closer it is to its natural state and the better it is.

STORING OLIVE OIL

Light and heat are oil's enemies. Keep olive oil in a cool and dark place, tightly sealed. This will assure your olive oil maintains its protective qualities, as well as its great taste. Oxygen promotes rancidity. Olive oil can easily go rancid when exposed to air, light or high temperatures.

HEALTH BENEFITS

Olive oil is a fat, so that begs the question, what makes it so good for you?

Olive oil is a monounsaturated fat, making it a good fat. Monounsaturated fats wipe out the wrong kind of cholesterol (LDL) and cheer on the good kind (HDL). In contrast, saturated and trans fats — such as butter, animal fats, tropical oils and partially hydrogenated oils — increase your risk of heart disease by increasing LDL cholesterol and decreasing the HDL variety. While all types of olive oil are sources of monounsaturated fat, extra virgin olive oil is the least processed variety and, therefore, it is the most heart healthy. According to the Food and Drug Administration (FDA), consuming about two tablespoons of olive oil a day may reduce your risk of heart disease. Because extra virgin olive oil is not refined, it retains higher levels of antioxidants and also contains vitamin E and phenols. It is believed that antioxidants can help protect you from developing many different kinds of cancer. In addition to being beneficial to your heart, there is evidence that women who consume olive oil more than once a day have lower risks of developing breast cancer. It has also been shown that olive oil lowers blood cholesterol levels, stimulates metabolism, promotes digestion, lubricates mucous membranes and lessens the severity of arthritis. In short, it is one of the most nutritious foods available. You can get the greatest health benefit by substituting olive oil for saturated fats, rather than just adding olive oil to a saturated fats-rich diet.

SEA SALT

The purpose of using salt in cooking is to extract and enhance flavor. Try, for example, eating a ripe tomato slice. Does it taste good on its own? Yes, I am sure it does. Now try the same tomato with just a touch of sea salt. The flavor has just gone from good to incredible! Allow the same slice of tomato to sit on a plate with a bit of sea salt on top. You will notice that in addition to drawing out flavor, the salt draws out moisture.

Without salt, food is bland. I find that people are timid with their salt and often do not add enough while cooking. There are, of course, those on the other side of the spectrum that add way too much and will always salt their food before even trying it. The only way to learn to season properly is to taste, then add, taste again, add some more, etc. Taste your food first. If it is bland, add some salt. Keep in mind — you can always add, but you cannot take away. While proper seasoning enhances your food, adding too much salt can keep you from tasting the true flavor of your food.

We often hear that salt is not good for our health. Is that true? The answer is that it depends on the type of salt.

Doctors often recommend that we decrease our salt consumption, but this is a very broad and general recommendation. Most often, our salt intake comes from regular table salt and processed foods. The problem is that our bodies do not really know what to do with processed salt. Years of processed salt intake can damage almost all areas of the body, such as the heart, kidneys, muscles and bones. Processed salt also causes water retention, makes us feel bloated and can increase high blood pressure in patients who are already hypertensive and those who have salt sensitive hypertension.

Here is the difference: Table salt is mined from underground salt deposits and is more heavily processed to eliminate trace minerals. It usually contains an anti-caking additive to prevent clumping and is primarily kiln-dried sodium chloride. This drying process strips and removes 82 of the 84 essential minerals found in salt. The final product is unnatural and hard on the body. Excess refined salt increases appetite and decreases bone density. Refined salt is made because it is more profitable, "prettier," more aesthetically appealing and does not spoil. White, powdery, easily pourable table salt is the result of a distinct trade-off between aesthetics and profitability and health.

Sea salt is completely natural. It is harvested the same way it was harvested thousands of years ago by French salt farmers. It is hand raked and left in the sun to dry. All of the trace and micro-nutrients are fully intact. The correct balance of sodium and chloride are present as well as iron, calcium, magnesium, manganese, potassium, zinc and 84 other trace and micro-nutrients. The various minerals present in sea salt help us to maintain a healthy balance of the various electrolytes in our bodies.

In contrast to the health problems associated with refined salt, sea salt has many health benefits, including relieving sinus congestion, regulating or lowering blood pressure, helping to promote a more restful sleep, balancing water in the body to help reduce water retention, dissolving kidney stones, balancing blood sugar and relieving and preventing muscle cramps. Sea salt also enables the liver, kidneys and adrenals to work much more efficiently and it can boost the immune system.

In terms of flavor, sea salt is a great alternative to table salt. The larger crystals have a more intense and flavorful quality, and sea salt can be found in different colors and varieties. Its chemical content is the same sodium chloride contained in table salt, but because of its larger size and more intense flavor, sea salt can be used in smaller amounts. Try sprinkling just a few crystals of sea salt on top of a dish on which you would normally use several shakes of table salt. You will find that the flavor is better and you are consuming a smaller amount of sodium.

The bottom line is that unrefined natural sea salt is as essential to life as oxygen, water, vitamins, proteins and essential fats. But, as with most pleasures in our daily diet, sea salt should also be consumed in conscious moderation.

Shopping for sea salt can get confusing, particularly in a specialty store. There are so many varieties; pink Himalayan, red, grey, black lava, smoked, etc. So which one should you buy? It can be fun to try different exotic sea salts as each has a distinctive texture, color and flavor. Feel free to experiment. But coarse sea salt is the only salt you need for everyday cooking. I keep a container next to the stove to add to water when I am blanching or cooking pasta. To season food while cooking, use a salt grinder filled with the coarse sea salt. Grinders specifically for sea salt can be purchased at most stores that sell kitchen supplies. You will also find plastic disposable sea salt grinders at your local grocery store.

PEPPER

Black pepper is more than simply a spice that accompanies salt. The medicinal benefits of black pepper reach beyond its taste and the way it enhances your foods. Black pepper helps to improve digestion and it works as an anti-inflammatory agent that reduces bacterial growth, particularly in the intestinal tract. In addition, black pepper is known to have a high amount of antioxidant properties, making it a cancer-fighting spice as well as a source of manganese, iron, potassium, vitamin C, vitamin K and dietary fiber. The good news is that all you need to do is put a little bit in your food every day.

You enhance the freshness of pepper and get the most health benefits from it when you grind it yourself. The outer skin of the peppercorn enhances metabolism and that promotes weight loss. Preparing ground pepper powder at home is better than buying ready-made pepper powder, which only retains its freshness for up to three months. On the other hand, whole peppercorns can keep their freshness indefinitely. For this reason, I highly recommend that you invest in a good pepper grinder.

GARLIC

In many of the recipes in the sauté and roast sections of this book, I call for garlic as an optional addition. I keep pureed garlic in my refrigerator and pull from it often. If you have a food processor on hand, this makes for a convenient way to add garlic to a dish without having to peel and chop it each time you need it.

Put ½ cup of garlic cloves and ¾ cup of extra virgin olive oil in a food processor. Puree until all the garlic is finely chopped. Store it in a glass container in your refrigerator for up to 2 months. Make sure there is always olive oil covering the garlic.

Aside from garlic's brilliant flavor and an unmistakable aroma we all love, it also has many health benefits. Garlic is one of the most valuable and versatile foods on the planet and is widely recognized as a health-enhancing supplement. It promotes the well-being of the cardio and immune systems with its antioxidant properties and helps maintain healthy blood circulation. One of garlic's most potent health benefits is its ability to enhance the body's immune cell activity. The active component in garlic is the sulfur compound called allicin. This chemical is released when garlic is chopped and it is quite a powerful antibiotic, which helps the body inhibit germ growth and reproduction. In fact, it is said that one milligram of allicin has the potency of 15 standard units of penicillin.

Consider adding garlic to your dishes, not only for its flavor, but for its health benefits as well.

COOKING METHODS: RECIPES   SAUTÉ

ROAST

GRILL

BLANCH

METHOD COOKING

There are many methods of cooking, most of which have been known since antiquity. These include baking, roasting, blanching, sautéing, poaching, frying, grilling, barbecuing, smoking, boiling, steaming and braising, among others. Even microwaving is a method. Various methods use differing levels of heat and moisture, and vary in cooking time. The method you choose will greatly affect the end result. Some methods are more appropriate for some foods than for others. The methods I've chosen are the four I feel are most practical to fit a busy lifestyle and the ones I use most often.

SAUTÉ

Sautéing is a method of cooking that uses a small amount of fat in a shallow pan over high heat. Ingredients are cut into uniform pieces or thinly sliced to facilitate fast, even cooking. Food that is sautéed is browned while preserving its texture, moisture and flavor. The word sauté literally means "jump," a description of the motion the ingredients make as they are being cooked.

In a sauté, all ingredients are heated at once and cooked quickly. To facilitate this, the ingredients are rapidly moved around in the pan, either by the use of a spatula or by repeatedly jerking the pan.

A sauté pan must have a large enough surface area to hold all of the food in one layer so that steam can escape — this keeps the ingredients from stewing and promotes the development of fond (the brown bits and pieces that get stuck to the bottom of the pan). Most pans sold specifically as sauté pans have a wide flat base and low sides to maximize the surface area available for heating.

Sautéing requires only enough fat to lightly coat the bottom of the pan. Too much fat will cause the food to fry rather than slide and will interfere with the development of fond. The food is spread across the hot fat in the pan while sautéing and is turned or tossed frequently for even cooking. But tossing or stirring the items in the pan by shaking the pan too often can cause the pan to cool and make the sauté take longer.

SAUTÉ NOTES

* Allow the pan to get hot (2 – 3 minutes) before adding oil or the food you are cooking. Never add anything to a cold pan. Starting with a cold pan will cause the vegetables or proteins to sweat and they will end up boiling in their own liquid rather than sautéing. Adding food to a cold pan is like putting food into a cold oven.

* Do not crowd the pan. If there is a lot of food to sauté and the pan is too small to accommodate everything, cook in batches.

* The smaller the cut, the faster the food will cook. If the cuts of vegetables, meat or fish are too large, they may need to be transferred into a 350 – 375 degree oven to finish cooking. This will also prevent the food from burning on the stovetop.

* Make sure everything you are working with is dry before you sauté. Drying all vegetables, meat and fish on paper towels before sautéing will ensure the food browns rather than boiling in its own liquid. You never want to add water or moisture to hot oil because it will dangerously spit.

* Use the suggested cooking times in the recipes as a guide only. Oven and stovetop type (electric vs. gas), temperatures and thickness of food vary from kitchen to kitchen. Begin to use your senses; watch, taste, touch and smell to determine doneness.

BRUSSELS SPROUTS

INGREDIENTS
1 lb. fresh Brussels sprouts
Olive Oil, Sea Salt & Pepper

TO PREP
Cut off the bottom stem of the Brussels sprouts and
remove the outer leaves. Using a paring knife, remove
the core and pull apart, separating the leaves.
(shown on page 110)

METHOD
1. Have the Brussels sprouts prepped and pulled apart
into leaves.
2. Heat the sauté pan on high heat (1 – 2 minutes).
3. Add a small amount of Olive Oil (about 2 – 3
tablespoons).
4. Add the Brussels sprouts.
5. Sauté quickly.
6. Season with Sea Salt & Pepper.

TIPS
* Roasted butternut squash (page 93) and sautéed
Brussels sprout leaves make an excellent pair.
* Minced garlic or caramelized onions can be added for
additional flavor, if desired, at Step 4.

BRUSSELS SPROUT LEAVES WITH BACON, CORN & ONIONS

SERVES 4 AS A SIDE DISH

INGREDIENTS
½ lb. bacon, cut into short strips*
1 small onion, sliced
**1 lb. Brussels sprouts, pulled apart
into leaves**
1 ear fresh corn, cut off the cob
Olive Oil, Sea Salt & Pepper

Sauté the bacon on medium heat until crisp. Increase
the heat to high. Add the onion and cook until caramel
colored, about 2 – 3 minutes. Add the Brussels sprout
leaves, sauté quickly (1 minute) and remove from heat.
Add the raw corn and season with Sea Salt & Pepper.
This is a great accompaniment for sautéed chicken (page
71), tilapia (page 63) and scallops (page 61) and also
makes an excellent Thanksgiving side dish.

Leave out bacon for vegan.

MUSHROOMS

INGREDIENTS

8 oz. mushrooms: crimini or baby bella (shitakes can also be used, but the woody stems must be removed.)
Olive Oil, Sea Salt & Pepper

TO PREP

Clean the mushrooms by wiping off any dirt with a paper towel. If there is an excessive amount of dirt, submerge in a bowl of water, then quickly remove with your hands and allow to dry on paper towels. Washing mushrooms is not ideal because mushrooms absorb water. But, in my opinion, it is better than eating dirt. Slice the mushrooms in half or in quarters, according to your liking, maintaining uniform thickness.

METHOD

1. Have the mushrooms cleaned, dry and cut uniformly.
2. Heat the sauté pan on high heat.
3. Add a small amount of Olive Oil, about 2 – 3 tablespoons.
4. Add the mushrooms.
5. Sauté quickly.
6. Season with Sea Salt & Pepper.

TIPS

* Mushrooms contain a lot of water, so make sure your pan is hot enough or they will end up stewing in their own liquid.
* Mushrooms also absorb a lot of oil, so, depending on the amount of mushrooms you are sautéing, you may need to add additional Olive Oil to finish cooking.
* If you have fresh thyme on hand, add a sprig to the mushrooms while they are sautéing.
* Minced garlic or caramelized onions can be added for additional flavor if desired after Step 5.

MUSHROOM & GOAT CHEESE TART

SERVES 4

INGREDIENTS

3 tablespoons Olive Oil
1 medium sweet onion
8 oz. mushrooms, cleaned and sliced
1 teaspoon chopped fresh thyme
½ cup goat cheese, crumbled (optional)
1 puff pastry sheet (about ½ lb.), cut in half
Sea Salt & Pepper to taste

Remove the puff pastry from the freezer and put in the refrigerator about 4 hours in advance, allowing it to defrost so that it can be unfolded. Preheat the oven to 350 degrees. Heat the sauté pan on high. Add the Olive Oil and onion and sauté for 5 minutes. Add mushrooms and fresh thyme and sauté for 1 minute. Season with Sea Salt & Pepper. Remove from heat and allow to cool. Unfold the puff pastry, cut each sheet in half and place on parchment paper on a sheet pan, allowing space in between both pieces. Brush the pastry with extra virgin Olive Oil. Place the sautéed mushrooms and onions down the center of the pastry and top with goat cheese. Leave the sides flat on the sheet pan. No need to turn the sides up around the filling because the pastry will puff up on the side when baked. Bake in a 350 degree oven until lightly browned, about 18 minutes. Cut each tart in half and serve with a mixed green salad for an easy lunch for 4.

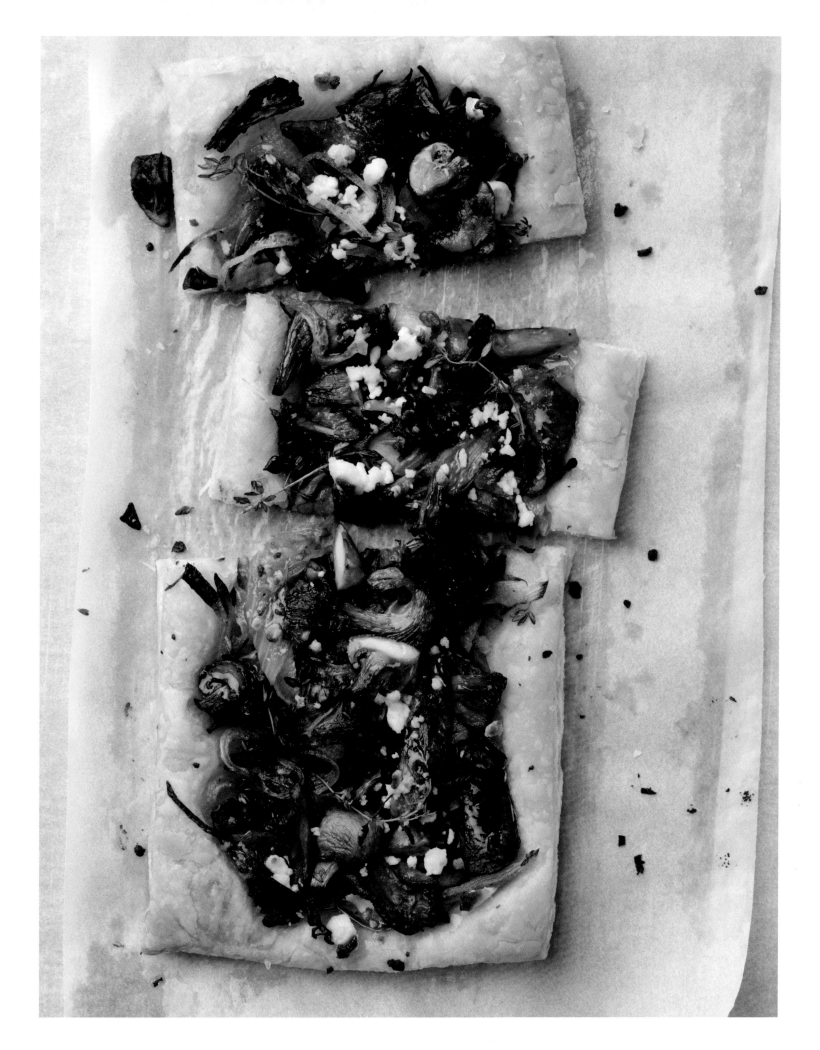

BUTTERNUT SQUASH

INGREDIENTS
1 butternut squash (about 1 ½ lbs.)
Olive Oil, Sea Salt & Pepper

TO PREP
Cut off top and bottom of the squash, then cut in half
where the neck ends and the round bottom begins.
Remove the outer skin with a peeler or a knife (I think a
knife is easier, but use whatever you are most comfortable with) and scoop out the inside of the round end
with a spoon. Small dice the squash into uniform pieces
to ensure even cooking.

METHOD
1. Have the butternut squash prepped and cut
uniformly.
2. Heat the sauté pan on high.
3. Add a small amount of Olive Oil to the pan (about
2 tablespoons).
4. Add the squash.
5. Sauté quickly. The squash should be slightly browned
on the outside and soft on the inside when done.
6. Season with Sea Salt & Pepper.

TIP
* The smaller the dice of the squash, the better. This will
allow it to cook faster. If you end up with a large cut, you
are better off roasting it (page 93) or transferring the
pan to a 350 degree oven to finish cooking.

BUTTERNUT SQUASH WITH LENTILS & ARUGULA

SERVES 4

INGREDIENTS
1 butternut squash, (1 ½ – 2 lbs.) prepped,
diced and sautéed as explained in
previous recipe
½ cup black beluga lentils
1 ½ cups water
1 tablespoon extra virgin Olive Oil
½ teaspoon garlic, minced
2 tablespoons red onion, small diced
2 cups baby arugula
Apple Cider Vinaigrette (page 178)
Sea Salt & Pepper to taste

Sauté butternut squash as described in previous recipe
and set aside. Cook lentils in 1 ½ cups of salted water
until all water is absorbed. Using 2 tablespoons of Olive
Oil, sauté minced garlic and red onion on medium heat
for 1 minute. Add the cooked lentils, remove from heat
and season with Sea Salt & Pepper (if needed). Plate
butternut squash and top with lentil mixture and baby
arugula. In a separate bowl prepare the Apple Cider
Vinaigrette as shown on page 178. Drizzle salad with
the vinaigrette.

ZUCCHINI & YELLOW SQUASH

INGREDIENTS
1 zucchini
1 yellow squash
Olive Oil, Sea Salt & Pepper

TO PREP
There are many ways to cut squash: into round disks, on
the bias (angle) to give it a longer oval shape or lengthwise with outer flesh cut off, seeds discarded and then
diced. Make sure your cuts are not too big. The thicker
the cut, the longer it will take to cook thoroughly.

METHOD
1. Have the squash cleaned, prepped and cut uniformly.
2. Heat the sauté pan on high.
3. Add a small amount of Olive Oil.
4. Add the squash.
5. Sauté quickly, about 2 minutes.
6. Season with Sea Salt & Pepper.

TIPS
* Minced garlic or caramelized onions can be added for
additional flavor if desired at Step 4.
* Patty pan squash can also be used. Cut into quarters
or eighths and cook the same way.

ZUCCHINI WITH LEEKS, PEAS & MINT

SERVES 2

INGREDIENTS
1 medium leek
1 zucchini
1 yellow squash
½ cup peas, blanched (page 171)
3 leaves fresh mint, julienned
Olive Oil (as needed)
Sea Salt & Pepper to taste

If you have access to a mandolin, this is a fun way to cut
squash. Remove the top and bottom of the squash, then
slice the outer flesh on the julienne setting of the mandolin until you get down to the seeds, then stop. Discard
center seeds.
Wash the leek thoroughly, making sure it is free of sand,
and julienne into long thin strips.
Sauté the leeks until soft (about 1 minute), then add the
squash. Sauté for an additional 2 – 3 minutes or until
cooked through. Season with Sea Salt & Pepper. Finish
with blanched peas and fresh mint.
Eat by itself or as a side with salmon (page 64). You can
also toss with cooked linguini and parmesan cheese to
create a pasta dish.

SWEET POTATOES

INGREDIENTS
1 large sweet potato
Olive Oil, Sea Salt & Pepper

TO PREP
Peel the sweet potato and remove the ends. Small dice by cutting the potato lengthwise into ½ inch slices. Then cut each slice lengthwise again into ½ inch sticks. Line up 6 sweet potato sticks and cut them one last time crosswise every ½ inch to create small ½ inch x ½ inch squares.

METHOD
1. Have the sweet potatoes prepped, cleaned and cut uniformly.
2. Heat the sauté pan on medium (for about 2 minutes).
3. Add a small amount of Olive Oil (start with 2 tablespoons).
4. Add the sweet potatoes.
5. Sauté about 10 minutes.
6. Season with Sea Salt & Pepper.

TIP
* Sweet potatoes contain natural sugars. Those sugars will caramelize quickly, so the sweet potatoes will brown and burn faster than other vegetables. The smaller cut will allow them to cook through more quickly. Keep an eye on your heat. You may need to lower it if the sweet potatoes are developing color too quickly, or you may need to finish cooking them in a 350 degree oven.

OVER EASY EGGS WITH SWEET POTATO HASH

SERVES 4

INGREDIENTS
2 large sweet potatoes, diced
1 small sweet onion, diced
1 cup red pepper, diced
½ lb. bulk turkey or pork sausage (omit to make vegetarian)
2 cups swiss chard, cut into strips
4 eggs
Olive Oil, Sea Salt & Pepper

Sauté sweet potatoes as explained in previous recipe until cooked through and set aside. In a separate pan, sauté onion in 1 tablespoon of Olive Oil on medium heat for 3 minutes. Add red pepper and turkey or pork sausage. Sauté until browned and cooked through, about 5 minutes. Add the swiss chard and cook for 1 additional minute. Remove from heat and add cooked sweet potatoes.

For the eggs, heat a nonstick sauté pan on medium for 1 minute. Spray lightly with non-stick cooking spray or Olive Oil. Add the eggs, cover and turn off the heat. Allow them to stay covered in the pan for 3 minutes. After 3 minutes, the white of the eggs should be cooked and the yolk should remain runny. Portion out hash onto 4 plates and top with 1 egg per plate.

FAJITAS

SERVES 8

INGREDIENTS

2 bell peppers, julienned
1 medium onion, sliced thin
8 flour tortillas
1 can black beans, drained and rinsed
1 cup sour cream
1 cup shredded jack cheese
2 cups guacamole
1 cup fresh salsa or pico de gallo
2 tablespoons Olive Oil
Sea Salt & Pepper

Heat the sauté pan on high and add 2 tablespoons of Olive Oil. Sauté the onions for 5 minutes on medium heat. Add the peppers, sauté for 1 – 2 minutes and season with Sea Salt & Pepper.
Display all the components (which can be purchased already prepared) individually and allow everyone to build their own fajitas.

TIPS

* To add chicken use 1 lb. chicken breast or boneless thigh meat, cut into strips (you may be able to purchase chicken already cut into strips). Get the sauté pan hot over high heat and add Olive Oil. Season chicken strips with Sea Salt & Pepper. Sauté the chicken strips in Olive Oil on high heat until browned and cooked through, about 3 – 5 minutes.
* Roasted chicken (page 119) pulled apart can also be used.
* To add beef use 1 ½ lbs of flank or skirt steak, cooked as explained on page 76. Allow meat to rest and slice thin.
* For burritos, add 2 cups of cooked brown rice to the lineup.

I like to keep all of these components in the refrigerator (especially when I have a busy week) for a quick lunch or dinner option. My kids assemble their own burritos and pack them for school lunches or make them as an after-school snack.

BELL PEPPERS

INGREDIENTS

1 bell pepper, any color
Olive Oil, Sea Salt & Pepper

TO PREP

Cut the outside of the pepper into 4 large pieces. Discard the stem, seeds and center. From here you can dice or julienne (cut into strips) the pepper easily.

METHOD

1. Have the pepper cleaned, prepped and cut uniformly.
2. Heat the sauté pan on high.
3. Add a small amount of Olive Oil.
4. Add the bell pepper.
5. Sauté quickly for about 2 minutes.
6. Season with Sea Salt & Pepper.

TIPS & SUGGESTIONS

* These sautéed peppers, along with onions, are perfect for omelets, fajitas or served with grilled sausages. All options work great for large groups.
* For grilled sausages with sautéed peppers and onions, serve with buns, Dijon or grainy mustard and a mixed green salad. One pepper and one onion will accommodate up to 8 sausages.

TOMATOES

INGREDIENTS

8 tomatoes, diced
2 teaspoons garlic, minced
3 – 5 fresh basil leaves, cut into strips
Olive Oil, Sea Salt & Pepper

TO PREP

Remove the stems from the tops of the tomatoes with a paring knife. Cut the tomato in half and roughly dice into smaller pieces.

METHOD

1. In a large sauté pan warm 3 tablespoons of Olive Oil with the minced garlic and allow to become fragrant (not brown).
2. Immediately add the chopped tomatoes and Sea Salt & Pepper.
3. Allow the tomatoes to break down, stirring occasionally for 10 minutes.
4. Remove from heat, add basil and season with Sea Salt & Pepper.
5. You can leave the sauce "chunky style" or puree in the food processor.

TIP

* This tomato sauce is ideal in the summertime, especially if you have a garden (or your neighbor has a garden) with an overabundance of tomatoes that have ripened all at once. The less-than-perfect looking tomatoes will make a delicious sauce. Another great time to make this is if you have leftover tomato salad. At Step 2, add the tomato salad and follow the same steps to finish. Use this sauce to make homemade pizzas or to toss with pasta.

PASTA WITH FRESH TOMATO SAUCE

SERVES 5

INGREDIENTS

1 lb. of pasta, linguini (or shape of your choice)
8 tomatoes, sautéed as explained in previous recipe
5 basil leaves, julienned
Extra virgin Olive Oil, Sea Salt & Pepper
¼ cup parmesan cheese, grated (optional)

Bring a medium pot of water to a hard boil. Add enough Sea Salt to the water so it tastes like the sea. Add the pasta and cook for 5 minutes (or as instructed until done). Strain the pasta in a colander and add to the tomato sauce. Toss to coat and finish with extra virgin Olive Oil and grated Parmesan cheese if desired. Season with Sea Salt & Pepper as needed.

RATATOUILLE

SERVES 8

INGREDIENTS
1 teaspoon garlic, minced
1 medium red onion, diced
2 zucchini, diced
2 yellow squash, diced
1 large eggplant, diced
1 red pepper, diced
8 plum tomatoes, diced
5 large leaves fresh basil, cut into strips
Olive Oil, Sea Salt & Pepper

Heat a large sauté pan on high. Add a small amount of Olive Oil (3 tablespoons). Add the garlic and onion and cook until soft, about 1 minute. Add the eggplant, season with Sea Salt & Pepper and sauté for 1 minute. Add 2 more tablespoons of Olive Oil to the pan and add the zucchini, yellow squash and peppers. Cook for 2 minutes. Season with Sea Salt & Pepper. Add the tomatoes and cook for an additional 3 minutes. Season again with Sea Salt & Pepper and finish with basil.

TIPS
* This is wonderful cold or hot. I like to make a big batch and keep it in the refrigerator to pull out for a quick lunch. Perfect with good crusty bread, or over a bowl of soft polenta, quinoa or brown rice.
* If you only have a small or medium sized sauté pan, sauté all components separately, then combine together after each ingredient is cooked.

ONIONS

INGREDIENTS
1 medium onion (sweet, Vidalia or yellow)
Olive Oil, Sea Salt & Pepper

TO PREP
Cut the top and bottom off the onion, then cut in half. Remove the skin and, with the flat side down, thinly slice the onion.

METHOD
1. Have the onions prepped and cut uniformly.
2. Heat the sauté pan on medium-high.
3. Add a small amount of Olive Oil (2 tablespoons).
4. Add the sliced onions.
5. Sauté for about 6 – 10 minutes, allowing the onion to break down and the color and flavor to develop.
6. Season with Sea Salt & Pepper.

TIPS
* If the onions are unevenly browning and drying out, add a little (1 – 3 teaspoons) water to the pan. This will keep them from burning and help to distribute the caramelized color evenly.
* Sautéed onions and caramelized onions have to be among my favorite additions to other vegetables. Onions contain natural sugars. When those sugars are cooked out, the onion develops a caramel color, hence the name "caramelized onions." Add these to any dish and I promise you will not be disappointed. Especially when working with bitter greens, the sweet onion is a great contrast. These onions are also an excellent addition to sandwiches. I list sautéed onions as an addition to all of the other vegetables in this section. If you are not a fan of raw onions, give the cooked caramelized version a try before ruling out this vegetable.

GREENS

INGREDIENTS

1 bunch of any of the following: kale, beet greens, collard greens, mustard greens, rainbow chard, Swiss chard or spinach
Olive Oil, Sea Salt & Pepper

TO PREP

Whether you are working with kale, beet greens, spinach or mustard greens, begin by making sure the greens are washed and free of any dirt or sand. The best way to wash greens is to submerge them in cold water and allow them to sit for 3 minutes so the dirt falls to the bottom. Remove the greens from the water, place in a colander and dry using a salad spinner. Repeat this process twice if they are extra gritty. (If you dump the water with the greens into a colander the dirt will be poured back onto the greens.) Large greens can be cut into strips. Do not worry about cutting the strips too small since they wilt and reduce. Thick stems on collard greens, mustard greens and kale should be removed. Rainbow chard and beet green stems can be left on, cut up with the leaves and sautéed.

METHOD

1. Have the greens cleaned and prepped as described above.
2. Heat the sauté pan on high.
3. Add a small amount of Olive Oil (start with 2 tablespoons).
4. Add the greens.
5. Sauté quickly. One minute for spinach and up to 3 minutes for other greens.
6. Season with Sea Salt & Pepper.

TIPS

* Minced garlic or caramelized onions can be added for additional flavor if desired at Step 2.
* Sautéed greens are excellent with cannellini beans or soft polenta.
* For a quick dinner, slice and toast a baguette or bread in the oven with Olive Oil and top with sautéed greens and a poached, fried or soft boiled egg — delicious!

SAUTÉED COLLARD GREENS WITH TURNIP & BACON

SERVES 5

INGREDIENTS

1 bunch collard greens, stems removed, cut into strips, washed and dried
½ lb. bacon, diced (optional)
1 cup turnip, peeled and diced into quarter inch cubes
1 medium onion, diced small
Olive Oil, Sea Salt & Pepper

Using a large sauté pan, add 1 tablespoon Olive Oil and the bacon. Cook on medium-low heat until crisp, about 5 minutes. Add the turnip and sauté for 1 minute, then add the onions and cook for 2 – 3 additional minutes. Add collard greens and cook for 3 – 5 minutes on medium-high heat. Season with Sea Salt & Pepper. This makes a great side dish for Thanksgiving.

HOW TO SAUTÉ:
CARROTS

INGREDIENTS
2 large carrots
Olive Oil, Sea Salt & Pepper

TO PREP
Remove the tops and bottoms of the carrots
and peel. You can either slice into round disks,
cut on the bias (diagonal slices) or julienne. To
julienne using a knife, start by making long thin
oval cuts, slicing the pieces diagonally. Then lay
the pieces flat in a row and cut into thin sticks.

METHOD
1. Have your carrots peeled, cleaned and
cut uniformly.
2. Heat your sauté pan on high.
3. Add a small amount of Olive Oil (about 2
tablespoons).
4. Add your carrots.
5. Sauté quickly, about 2 minutes.
6. Season with Sea Salt & Pepper.

TIP
* Carrots can also be purchased precut in a bag
in your grocer's produce section. This can be a
great timesaver!

POTATOES

INGREDIENTS
1 lb. Yukon Gold potatoes
Olive Oil, Sea Salt & Pepper

TO PREP
Small to medium dice the potatoes. After they are cut, store the diced potatoes in cold water to keep them from browning and to remove some of the starch. They can be cut a day ahead of time and stored in the refrigerator under water until needed. Drain and dry with a kitchen towel thoroughly before sautéing.

METHOD
1. Have the potatoes prepped, dry and cut uniformly.
2. Heat the sauté pan on medium-high.
3. Add a small amount of Olive Oil (start with 3 tablespoons).
4. Add the potatoes.
5. Sauté quickly, about 10 minutes, until potatoes are cooked through and browned on the outside.
6. Season with Sea Salt & Pepper and drizzle with extra virgin Olive Oil.

TIP
* Add fresh rosemary and crushed garlic while sautéing the potatoes for additional flavor at Step 3.

POTATO HASH

SERVES 4

INGREDIENTS
2 large Yukon Gold potatoes, sautéed as
explained in previous recipe
½ sweet onion, diced
1 red bell pepper, diced
2 tablespoons parsley, chopped
Olive Oil, Sea Salt & Pepper

Prepare potatoes as directed above and set aside. In a large sauté pan, cook the onions on medium heat in 2 tablespoons of Olive Oil for 1 – 2 minutes. Add the diced red pepper and the cooked potatoes. Sauté for an additional 2 minutes. Season and serve.

* This is wonderful as a side dish for breakfast or brunch.

SAUTÉED CARROTS, SHITAKES & ZUCCHINI

SERVES 4 AS A SIDE DISH

INGREDIENTS

   1 medium onion, sliced
   1 clove garlic, minced
   6 oz. shitake mushrooms, stems removed
   and cut into strips
   2 carrots, julienned
   1 zucchini, cut into long spaghetti strips
   using a mandolin (page 44)
   Olive Oil, Sea Salt & Pepper

Heat a large sauté pan over high heat for one minute.
Add 2 tablespoons of Olive Oil and the sliced onion.
Cook for 1 minute, then add the garlic and cook for
an additional 1 – 2 minutes. Add the shitakes, season
with Sea Salt & Pepper and sauté for 1 minute. Add the
carrots and zucchini and cook for 1 additional minute.
Season with Sea Salt & Pepper.

* Excellent by itself, with brown rice or with sautéed
halibut (page 67).
* This can also be tossed with a half-pound of cooked
linguini and finished with extra virgin Olive Oil and
fresh basil.

SCALLOPS

INGREDIENTS

**Scallops, 3 – 4 "U/10*" size per person,
or 6 oz. per person**
Olive Oil, Sea Salt & Pepper
½ lemon

TO PREP

Make sure scallops are dry (place between paper towels if needed) with the small muscle found on the side of each scallop removed.

METHOD

1. Make sure scallops are prepped as described above.
2. Season well on both sides with Sea Salt & Pepper.
3. Heat the sauté pan on high (2 minutes).
4. Add a small amount of Olive Oil (about 1 – 2 tablespoons).
5. Place the scallops in the pan and allow to brown on each side for about 2 – 3 minutes per side.
6. As the scallops reach the desired doneness, squeeze half of a lemon over them. Allow the liquid to reduce to form a sauce and remove pan from heat.
7. Plate the scallops and drizzle with high quality extra virgin Olive Oil and sauce from the pan.

*U/10 is a reference to size. "U" stands for "under," indicating that it will take fewer than 10 to make up a pound. The smaller the number is, the larger (by weight) the scallops are. U/10 are the biggest ones available.

SCALLOPS WITH ARUGULA SALAD & LEMON VINAIGRETTE

SERVES 2

INGREDIENTS

12 oz. scallops
3 oz. baby arugula
Lemon-Dijon Vinaigrette (page 178)
Sea Salt & Pepper to taste

Prepare the scallops as explained in previous recipe. In a bowl, season the arugula with Sea Salt & Pepper and dress with enough vinaigrette to coat the greens. To serve, divide the salad and scallops and plate.

TILAPIA

INGREDIENTS
1 piece tilapia
Olive Oil, Salt and Pepper
½ lemon

TO PREP
Rinse off the tilapia under cold water, then dry well using paper towels before cooking.

METHOD
1. Have the tilapia prepped as described above.
2. Season well on flesh side with Sea Salt & Pepper.
3. Heat the sauté pan on high.
4. Add a small amount of Olive Oil.
5. Place the tilapia in the pan and allow to brown on each side for 2 minutes per side.
6. Squeeze half a lemon over the fish and in the pan.
7. Plate the tilapia and drizzle with high quality extra virgin Olive Oil.

TIP
* Tilapia works great for fish tacos. Buy flour tortillas, green cabbage sliced thin, pico de gallo and sour cream mixed with some lime juice and you have a quick and easy taco Tuesday dinner.

TILAPIA WITH ARUGULA, SHAVED FENNEL & KALAMATA OLIVES

SERVES 2

INGREDIENTS
2 pieces tilapia, sautéed as explained in previous recipe
⅛ cup kalamata olives, pitted and cut in half
½ cup fennel, shaved and stored in cold water until ready to use
3 oz. baby arugula
Lemon-Dijon Vinaigrette (page 178)
Sea Salt & Pepper to taste

In a large bowl, combine the olives, shaved fennel and arugula. Season with Sea Salt & Pepper and dress with enough vinaigrette to coat the greens. Prepare the tilapia as described above and plate next to the salad to serve.

SALMON

INGREDIENTS

1 lb. salmon
Olive Oil, Sea Salt & Pepper

TO PREP

Salmon can be cooked in one large piece or in individual portions. I recommend cooking the salmon with the skin off, but you can certainly leave it on while cooking. To remove the skin, lay the salmon skin side down on the cutting board. Using a large chef's knife, place the blade in between the skin and the flesh of the salmon with the top of the knife angled toward you. Hold the knife firmly in place and with the other hand pull the skin toward you and push your knife away from you. The skin should separate easily from the rest of the salmon. Rinse off under cold water, then dry well using paper towels.

METHOD

1. Have the salmon dry with skin removed as described above.
2. Season well on both sides with Sea Salt & Pepper.
3. Heat the sauté pan on high and allow the pan at least 3 minutes to get hot.
4. Add a small amount of Olive Oil (about 1 tablespoon).
5. Place the salmon, flesh-side down, in the pan and allow to brown for 3 minutes. Turn it over to the skin side and allow to cook for 1 minute on high heat. Then turn the heat off, leaving the salmon in the pan to slowly carry-over cook for 5 – 10 minutes. The salmon should be slightly underdone in the center. If you prefer your salmon more done, cook on the second side for 2 minutes before turning the heat off. You can also place the sauté pan with the salmon into a 350 degree oven to cook through, or just to heat right before serving (2 – 3 minutes).
6. Plate the salmon and drizzle with high quality extra virgin Olive Oil.

TIPS

* Cooking time depends on the thickness of the salmon. The timing above is for a 1 inch thick piece.
* I much prefer the thicker cuts that are closer to the head side of the fish than the thin tail-end cuts. Thinner cuts are easier to overcook and may require even less cooking time per side.
* You can serve with the suggested salad below, vegetables from previous pages or top with barbeque sauce as shown on page 143.

SAUTÉED SALMON WITH SALAD & CUCUMBER DRESSING

SERVES 4

INGREDIENTS

1 lb. salmon, sautéed as explained in previous recipe
3 cups sourdough bread, medium diced (for croutons)
4 oz. green beans, blanched (page 159), cut in half into 2 inch pieces
1 avocado, diced
1/8 cup sunflower seeds
2 eggs, hard boiled, peeled and quartered (page 68)
2 heads bibb lettuce
2 – 3 tablespoons extra virgin Olive Oil
Sea Salt & Pepper to taste
Cucumber Dressing (page 179)

Preheat oven to 350 degrees. Toss diced sourdough in a bowl with 2 – 3 tablespoons extra virgin Olive Oil & Sea Salt. Toast croutons for 8 – 10 minutes or until lightly browned. Remove from the oven and allow to cool.
In a large bowl, combine the green beans, avocado, sunflower seeds and lettuce. Dress with the cucumber dressing, adding just enough to lightly coat everything. Season with Sea Salt & Pepper. Flake pieces of salmon on top of the salad along with the croutons and hard boiled egg.

GROUPER

INGREDIENTS

Grouper, 6 oz. per person
Olive Oil, Sea Salt & Pepper
½ lemon

TO PREP

Rinse off the grouper under cold water, then dry well using paper towels before cooking.

METHOD

1. Have the grouper prepped as described above.
2. Season well on both sides with Sea Salt & Pepper.
3. Heat the sauté pan on high.
4. Add a small amount of Olive Oil (1 – 2 tablespoons).
5. Place the grouper in the pan and allow to brown on each side for 3 – 5 minutes.
6. Squeeze half a lemon over the fish and into the pan.
7. Plate the grouper and drizzle with high quality extra virgin Olive Oil.

TIP

* If the pieces of grouper are thick, brown on both sides for 2 minutes, then finish cooking in a 375 degree oven for 5 minutes.

GROUPER WITH ASIAN SALAD

SERVES 2

INGREDIENTS

12 oz. grouper, sautéed as explained in previous recipe
1 carrot, julienned
½ cucumber, julienned
2 radishes, sliced thin
½ Asian pear, julienned
1 head bibb lettuce, torn into small pieces
Ginger-Soy Vinaigrette (page 179)

In a large bowl, combine the carrot, cucumber, radishes, pear and lettuce. Dress the salad with enough vinaigrette to coat the greens. Prepare the grouper as described above. To serve, divide the grouper and salad evenly and plate.

HALIBUT

INGREDIENTS

6 – 8 oz. halibut per person
½ lemon
Olive Oil, Sea Salt & Pepper

TO PREP

Rinse off the halibut under cold water, then dry well using paper towels before cooking. This will ensure it browns instead of stewing in its own liquid.

METHOD

1. Have the halibut dried as described above.
2. Season well on both sides with Sea Salt & Pepper.
3. Heat the sauté pan on high.
4. Add a small amount of Olive Oil (1 – 2 tablespoons).
5. Place the halibut in the pan and allow to brown on each side for 3 – 5 minutes.
6. Squeeze half a lemon over the fish and into the pan.
7. Plate the halibut and drizzle with high-quality extra virgin Olive Oil and juices from the pan.

SAUTÉED HALIBUT WITH KALE SALAD

SERVES 2

INGREDIENTS

2 6-ounce portions halibut, sautéed as explained in previous recipe
2 tablespoon extra virgin Olive Oil
2 large cloves garlic, thinly sliced
2 tablespoons currants
2 tablespoons toasted pine nuts
4 cups (packed) kale (red kale if available), thick stems removed and cut or torn into small bite-size pieces
¹/₈ cup shaved parmesan cheese (shaved with a peeler)
1 tablespoon balsamic vinegar
Sea Salt & Pepper to taste

Heat the oven to 350 degrees. Place the thinly sliced garlic in a small sauté pan with the extra virgin Olive Oil. Place in the oven for about 5 minutes or until lightly browned. Check the garlic halfway through and rotate around in the pan for even browning. Remove from the oven, add the currants and allow to cool. In a separate pan, toast the pine nuts by placing them on a sheet pan and baking them in the oven until lightly browned, about 5 – 8 minutes. They brown quickly, so as soon as you smell them they are ready. In a bowl combine the kale, pine nuts, balsamic vinegar, currents, garlic and all of the oil from the pan. Season with Sea Salt & Pepper and toss. Top with shaved parmesan cheese. To serve, plate the salad next to the halibut.

TUNA

INGREDIENTS

1 lb. sushi grade tuna (each steak should be about 1 ½ – 2 inches thick)
Olive Oil, Sea Salt & Pepper

TO PREP

To prep tuna you will need to remove the bloodline. Most of the time when you purchase fresh tuna the bloodline is already removed. If it's not, simply cut off the very dark part of the tuna located only on one side. Pat it dry and you are ready to cook!

METHOD

1. Have the tuna dry with dark bloodline removed.
2. Season heavily on both sides with Sea Salt & Pepper.
3. Heat the sauté pan on very high heat, allowing 3 minutes for the pan to get hot.
4. Add a small amount of Olive Oil (1 – 2 tablespoons).
5. Place the tuna in the pan and allow to brown on each side for up to 1 minute per side, depending on its thickness.
6. The tuna should be rare inside with the outside seared and crisp or you can continue cooking the tuna according to your preference. It will continue to cook, so immediately transfer it to a plate, then into the freezer for about 5 – 10 minutes to stop carryover cooking. (Don't forget it's in there!)
7. Slice the tuna into thin strips after it cools. This can be done hours in advance if needed. Store in the refrigerator until it is ready to serve.

TIP

* Use a very sharp knife when slicing tuna. If you do not, it will fall apart. Use a serrated knife to cut if you do not have a sharp knife. Do not bear down; just glide back and forth gently.

SEARED TUNA WITH SALAD NICOISE

SERVES 3

INGREDIENTS

1 lb. tuna, seared and sliced as explained in previous recipe
2 eggs
6 oz. small red potatoes, halved
1 tomato, diced
4 oz. green beans, blanched (page 159)
9 anchovies
¼ cup Niçoise olives, halved
Sea Salt & Pepper to taste
Mustard Vinaigrette (page 178)

Prepare tuna as previously described, slice and store in the refrigerator. Cook the eggs by placing them in a small pot with enough water to cover them. Cover the pot with a lid and bring water to a boil over medium-high heat. When the water comes to a boil, turn off the heat, leave the pot covered and let stand for 17 minutes. Remove the eggs from the hot water and place in a cold water bath. Peel off the shell and cut into quarters. Place the diced potatoes in another pot, cover with water and add some Sea Salt (about a tablespoon). Bring water to a boil and cook for about 5 minutes or until potatoes can easily be pierced with a knife. Strain them into a colander and allow to cool.

To plate, divide all the components evenly onto 3 plates, drizzle with enough vinaigrette to coat and serve.

CHICKEN

INGREDIENTS

2 chicken breasts, bone in, skin on (skinless, boneless is fine too)
Olive Oil, Sea Salt & Pepper

TO PREP

Trim off any excess fat from the chicken breast and dry well using paper towels.

METHOD

1. Preheat the oven to 375 degrees.
2. Have the chicken trimmed and dry.
3. Heat the sauté pan on high for 1 – 2 minutes.
4. Season chicken well on both sides with Sea Salt & Pepper.
5. Add a small amount of Olive Oil to the sauté pan (about 2 tablespoons).
6. Place the chicken in the pan, skin side down first, and allow to brown on each side for 2 – 3 minutes.
7. After browning, if using a boneless breast, place it in a 375 degree oven for 5 – 7 minutes or until cooked through. If it is a bone-in breast, it will need up to 20 minutes in the oven. Cooking time will vary depending on the thickness and size of the breast.
8. Remove from the oven and allow the meat to rest for 10 minutes. It will continue to cook and the juices will distribute within the meat. Allow the meat to rest before slicing or all of the juices will run out, resulting in a dry chicken. If, after the meat rests, you slice it and want it to be more cooked, place the sauté pan with the chicken in a 375 degree oven for an additional 5 minutes or until cooked through.
9. Drizzle with natural juices from the pan or extra virgin Olive Oil and serve.

TIPS

* You can remove the skin after cooking, but for a moist breast, it is better to keep the skin on while cooking.
* Sautéed chicken pairs well with blanched broccoli (page 165) or roasted broccoli (page 99) as a side dish.

SAUTÉED CHICKEN WITH DATE & WALNUT SALAD

SERVES 2

INGREDIENTS

2 chicken breasts, bone in and sautéed as explained in previous recipe
¼ cup walnuts, toasted
4 cups mixed greens
6 dates, quartered
¼ cup ricotta salata cheese, shaved (parmesan can also be used)
Sea Salt & Pepper to taste
Balsamic Vinaigrette (page 179)

Prepare the chicken as previously described and set aside to rest. Place the walnuts on a sheet pan and drizzle with about a teaspoon of Olive Oil, toss to coat. Toast in a 350 degree oven for 5 – 8 minutes. Remove from the oven and allow to cool. Place the mixed greens, dates and walnuts in a large bowl. Season with Sea Salt & Pepper and drizzle with enough vinaigrette to coat. Top with shaved ricotta salata. Serve the salad along with the chicken.

DUCK

INGREDIENTS

2 duck breasts
Olive Oil, Sea Salt & Pepper

TO PREP

Trim the fat to the shape of the meat. Then using the tip of your knife, score the fat by making diagonal slits into it in ½ inch intervals. Be careful not cut into breast meat. Rotate breast and score again in the opposite direction, making a criss-cross or diamond pattern on the fat.

METHOD

1. Have the duck breast trimmed and dry.
2. Season well on both sides with Sea Salt & Pepper.
3. Heat the sauté pan on medium-high (2 minutes).
4. Add a small amount of Olive Oil (2 teaspoons).
5. Place duck in the pan skin side down and allow to brown for 5 minutes, then turn and cook the other side for about 3 minutes.
6. Turn off the heat and allow the meat to rest for 10 minutes. It will continue to cook and the juices will distribute within the meat. Allow the meat to rest before slicing or all of the juices will run out, resulting in a dry duck breast.
7. If you want the meat to be cooked more after it has rested and been sliced, place the sauté pan with the duck in a 375 degree oven for 5 minutes or until it is cooked to your liking.

SAUTÉED DUCK BREAST WITH MANCHEGO CHEESE, DRIED CHERRY & PECAN SALAD

SERVES 2

INGREDIENTS

2 duck breasts, sautéed as explained in previous recipe
⅛ cup pecans, toasted
4 cups mixed baby greens
⅛ cup dried cherries
¼ cup manchego cheese, shaved (using a peeler)
2 – 3 teaspoons balsamic vinegar
2 tablespoons extra virgin Olive Oil
Sea Salt & Pepper

Prepare the duck as previously described, set aside and allow to rest. Heat the oven to 375 degrees. Place the pecans on a sheet pan and drizzle with about a teaspoon of Olive Oil, toss to coat. Toast the pecans for 5 – 8 minutes or until fragrant and browned. Remove from the oven and let cool. In a large bowl, combine the mixed greens, cherries and pecans. Season with Sea Salt & Pepper and dress the greens with balsamic vinegar and extra virgin Olive Oil. To serve, slice the duck into 5 pieces on the diagonal and plate next to the salad. Top salad with shaved manchego cheese.

LAMB

INGREDIENTS
1 rack of lamb, frenched
Olive Oil, Sea Salt & Pepper

TO PREP
You should be able to purchase your rack of lamb "frenched" from the butcher. This simply means that the rib bones are exposed by cutting off the fat and meat that covers them. Trim off any excess fat from the rack of lamb and dry well using paper towels.

METHOD
1. Preheat oven to 375 degrees.
2. Season lamb well on all sides with Sea Salt & Pepper.
3. Heat the sauté pan on high.
4. Add a small amount of Olive Oil (1 – 2 tablespoons).
5. Place the lamb in the pan and allow to brown on each side for 3 – 5 minutes.
6. Transfer the sauté pan with the meat to the oven and cook for 5 – 10 minutes or to your liking. Cook time will depend in the thickness of the lamb rack. Remove from the oven and allow to rest for 10 – 20 minutes. It will continue to cook and the juices will distribute within the meat. Allow the meat to rest before slicing or all of the juices will run out, resulting in dry lamb.
7. After the meat rests, slice between each bone into individual chops. Drizzle with natural juices from the pan or extra virgin Olive Oil and serve.

TIP
* If you want the meat to be more cooked after it rests and you slice it, place the sauté pan with the lamb in a 375 degree oven for 5 minutes or until it is cooked to your liking.

LAMB CHOPS WITH GREEK SALAD

SERVES 2

INGREDIENTS
1 rack of lamb, sautéed as in previous recipe
1 head romaine lettuce
1 tomato, diced
¼ cup kalamata olives, pitted and halved
½ cucumber, peeled and diced
¼ cup feta, crumbled
3 – 5 mint leaves, chiffonade (cut into thin strips)
Sea Salt & Pepper to taste
Red Wine Dijon Vinaigrette (page 179)

Prepare the lamb as previously described. Cut the romaine into ½ inch strips, wash in cold water and dry in a salad spinner. In a large bowl, combine the romaine, tomato, olives, cucumber, feta and mint. Dress with enough Dijon Vinaigrette to lightly coat the greens. Season salad with Sea Salt & Pepper and plate next to the lamb.

HANGER STEAK

INGREDIENTS
1 lb. hanger steak, trimmed
Olive Oil, Sea Salt & Pepper

TO PREP
Trim off any excess fat from the hanger steak and dry on paper towels if needed.

METHOD
1. Have the steak trimmed and dry.
2. Season well on both sides with Sea Salt & Pepper.
3. Heat the sauté pan on high (2 minutes).
4. Add a small amount of Olive Oil (1 tablespoon).
5. Place the steak in the pan and allow to brown on all 3 sides for 2 – 3 minutes per side.
6. Continue cooking the meat to slightly under the doneness you like. Turn off the heat and allow the meat to rest in the pan for 10 – 20 minutes. It will continue to cook and the juices will distribute within the meat. Allow the meat to rest before slicing or all of the juices will run out, resulting in a dry steak.
7. If you find that you want the meat more cooked after it rests and you slice it, place the sauté pan with the steak in a 375 degree oven for 5 minutes or until the meat is cooked to your liking.
8. Drizzle with natural juices from the pan or extra virgin Olive Oil and serve.

TIPS
* This same method can be used with different cuts of beef: NY strip, T-bone, skirt and tenderloin.
* Cooking time will vary depending on the thickness of the cut.

HANGER STEAK WITH SAUTÉED MUSHROOMS

SERVES 2

INGREDIENTS
1 hanger steak 12 – 14 ounces, sautéed as explained in previous recipe
6 oz. mushrooms, shitake or crimini, sliced
Olive Oil, Sea Salt & Pepper

Remove the steak from the sauté pan once it is cooked. Return the pan to a high heat, add the mushrooms and allow to cook in the juices and remaining oil (add more oil if needed) for 2 minutes. There should be enough salt and pepper remaining in the pan to season the mushrooms as well. To serve, slice the steak and top with the mushrooms.

PORK

INGREDIENTS
2 pork chops, trimmed
Olive Oil, Sea Salt & Pepper

TO PREP
Trim off any excess fat from the pork chops and dry well using paper towels.

METHOD
1. Have the pork chops trimmed and dry.
2. Season well on both sides with Sea Salt & Pepper.
3. Heat the sauté pan on high.
4. Add a small amount of Olive Oil (1 – 2 tablespoons).
5. Place the pork in the pan and allow to brown for 3 – 5 minutes on each side (depending on the thickness).
6. Continue cooking the meat to slightly under the doneness you like. Turn off the heat and allow the meat to rest in the pan for 10 minutes. It will continue to cook and the juices will distribute within the meat. Allow the meat to rest before slicing or all of the juices will run out, resulting in dry pork.
7. If you want the meat more cooked after it has rested and you slice it, place the sauté pan with the chops in a 375 degree oven for 5 minutes or until they are cooked to your liking.

TIP
* Pork pairs well with roasted butternut squash (page 43) and sautéed Brussels sprout greens (page 39).

PORK WITH PEAR, BLUE CHEESE & WALNUT SALAD

SERVES 2

INGREDIENTS
2 pork chops, sautéed as explained in previous recipe
¼ cup walnuts, toasted
1 Bartlett pear
4 cups mixed baby greens
2 tablespoons crumbled blue cheese
Balsamic Vinaigrette (page 179)
Sea Salt & Pepper to taste

Prepare the pork as in previous recipe and set aside to rest. Place the walnuts on a sheet pan and drizzle with about a teaspoon of Olive Oil, toss to coat. Toast in a 375 degree oven for 5 – 8 minutes. Remove from the oven and allow to cool. Cut the pear by cutting it in quarters from top to bottom. Lay each quarter on its side and cut out the core. Then cut each quarter into 3 wedges. Place the mixed greens, pear and walnuts in a large bowl. Season with Sea Salt & Pepper and drizzle with enough vinaigrette to coat. Top with crumbled blue cheese. Serve the salad along with the pork.

ROAST

To roast is to cook with indirect dry heat in an oven.

I love the idea of roasting vegetables in the oven. It is easy, hands-free cooking and virtually goof-proof (so long as you do not forget to take the food out of the oven!). You can prepare vegetables days in advance or save prep time by buying already prepped vegetables, such as pre-cut broccoli florets, butternut squash in a bag or peeled baby carrots. This allows you to do other things while dinner is in the oven.

ROAST NOTES

* When roasting, always use a sheet pan (cookie sheet) with sides.

* It is a good idea to remove the pan from the oven once or twice while roasting, moving the vegetables around to ensure even cooking.

* Remember, the cooking times in this section are "suggested times." Because of variations in size and oven temperature, the times should be used as a general guide only.

* The temperatures in this section were based on convection oven temperatures. If your oven is not convection, set it on bake and just know that it will take longer than the suggested roasting times stated in the recipe.

* If you have more than one item in the oven this will also extend the cooking time.

ONION

INGREDIENTS
1 sweet onion

METHOD
1. Wrap the onion with skin on in tin foil and place in a 350 degree oven for 2 hours or until you can pierce the onion all the way through easily with a knife.
2. Remove from oven and allow to cool for about an hour.
3. Cut off top and bottom, remove outer skin, cut in half and julienne.

TIP:
* Many people avoid raw onions because they cause stomach irritation due to the gasses they contain. When onions are cooked they no longer release these gasses. Roasting the whole onion is an excellent way to enjoy this vegetable in salads, on sandwiches or on burgers without the upset stomach.

ROASTED ONION & PINE NUT SALAD

SERVES 4 AS A SIDE DISH

INGREDIENTS
**1 onion, roasted and julienned
as described in previous recipe
3 tablespoons extra virgin Olive Oil
1 tablespoon red or white wine vinegar
¼ cup pine nuts, toasted
2 teaspoons fresh sage, chopped
Sea Salt & Pepper to taste**

Place the pine nuts on a sheet pan, drizzle with about 1 teaspoon of Olive Oil and toss to coat. Toast in a 350 degree oven for 5 – 8 minutes or until lightly browned. Remove from the oven and allow to cool. Combine all ingredients in a bowl and mix well. Season with Sea Salt & Pepper. Can be made a day in advance. This is an excellent accompaniment to any fish.

BEETS

INGREDIENTS
1 bunch red or gold beets
Olive Oil, Sea Salt & Pepper

TO PREP
Wash beets to remove all sand and dirt and remove tops.

METHOD
1. Preheat oven to 375 degrees.
2. Wrap beets all together (not individually) in aluminum foil. Be sure not to have any holes in the aluminum foil (this will allow steam to escape).
3. Place on a sheet pan and roast in the oven. Roast for about 45 minutes for baby beets and 60 – 90 minutes or longer for larger beets, depending on the size. You can check for doneness by sticking them with a paring knife. When the knife slides in and out easily, they are thoroughly cooked.
4. Open the foil and allow them to cool.
5. Using a paring knife, cut a little off the top of each beet. Then, using your fingers, peel the skin off of the beet. It should come off easily.
6. Leave whole or cut up and store in the refrigerator. To serve, drizzle diced beets with good extra virgin Olive Oil, Sea Salt & Pepper.

TIPS
* If you are roasting both yellow and red beets, wrap them separately. If not, the red will bleed onto the gold.
* For a great appetizer, create bruschetta with toasted bread (explained on page 104), spread with soft goat cheese and top with diced beets.

ROASTED BEETS WITH ARUGULA & BURRATA SALAD

SERVES 4
AS A FIRST COURSE OR SIDE SALAD

INGREDIENTS
1 bunch beets, roasted as explained in previous recipe, peeled and large diced
12 – 16 oz. burrata cheese (similar to fresh mozzarella)
3 oz. baby arugula or frisée
Extra virgin Olive Oil, Sea Salt & Pepper

Divide roasted beets, burrata and arugula among 4 plates. Drizzle with extra virgin Olive Oil and season with Sea Salt & Pepper.

POTATOES

INGREDIENTS
1 ½ lbs. fingerling potatoes
Olive Oil, Sea Salt & Pepper

TO PREP
I prefer to use fingerling potatoes if available. I also like the small or large Yukon Gold potatoes to roast. Cut the fingerlings in half if medium sized, into quarters for larger ones or leave whole if they are really small. Try to keep the cuts uniform to ensure even cooking. Potatoes can be cut up to a day in advance and kept in the refrigerator submerged in water. Drain and dry potatoes on a towel before roasting.

METHOD
1. Preheat the oven to 375 degrees.
2. Have the potatoes prepped and cut uniformly, as described above.
3. Place the potatoes in a bowl, then toss and coat with Olive Oil, Sea Salt & Pepper.
4. Place on a sheet pan with fresh rosemary and roast in the oven for 35 – 40 min. After 25 minutes, remove the pan from the oven and, using a spatula, rotate the potatoes to ensure even cooking. Return to the oven.
5. The potatoes should be soft all the way through and browned when done.
6. Drizzle with good extra virgin Olive Oil and season with additional Sea Salt & Pepper if needed.

TIP
* These are always such a hit in our house. They barely make it from the pan to the plate! My daughter treats them as French fries. My son and I love them in a bowl with roasted broccoli (page 99). They also are perfect with strip steak (page 148) for meat and potato lovers.

FENNEL

INGREDIENTS

1 fennel bulb
$^1/_3$ lb. pancetta or bacon, sliced (optional)
Olive Oil, Sea Salt & Pepper

TO PREP

Remove the tops of the fennel, saving some of the fronds for later use. Cut the bulb in half and remove the bottom core. Slice each bulb lengthwise into uniform 1 inch pieces.

METHOD

1. Preheat the oven to 375 degrees.
2. Have the fennel prepped and cut uniformly as described above.
3. Place the fennel in a bowl, then toss and coat evenly with Olive Oil, Sea Salt & Pepper.
4. Place on a sheet pan along with pancetta or bacon (optional) and roast in the oven for 20 – 25 minutes. Remove pan from oven halfway through the cooking time and move the fennel and pancetta around to ensure even cooking.
5. The fennel should be soft all the way through and the pancetta should be crisp when done. The best way to check for doneness is to pull a piece off the tray, allow it to cool and taste it.

TIPS

* Excellent served along with sautéed scallops (page 61) with or without the pancetta or bacon.
* See couscous recipe on page 101, made with roasted fennel.

ROASTED FENNEL, PEACH & PANCETTA SALAD

SERVES 2

INGREDIENTS

1 bulb fennel, sliced
$^1/_3$ pound pancetta or bacon (optional), roasted with fennel as explained in previous recipe
3 oz. arugula
1 peach, sliced into wedges (or pears, depending on the season)
2 tablespoons Balsamic Vinaigrette (page 179)
Extra virgin Olive Oil
Sea Salt & Pepper

Divide the peaches, arugula, fennel and pancetta or bacon evenly on 2 plates. Drizzle with Balsamic Vinaigrette and serve.

RUTABAGAS

INGREDIENTS
2 rutabagas
Olive Oil, Sea Salt & Pepper

TO PREP
Remove the thick, sometimes waxy outer skin with a paring knife. Cut the rutabagas in half and then large dice.

METHOD
1. Preheat the oven to 350 degrees.
2. Have the rutabagas prepped and cut uniformly as described above.
3. Place the rutabagas in a bowl, then toss and coat with Olive Oil, Sea Salt & Pepper.
4. Place on a sheet pan and roast in the oven for 30 – 45 min. After 25 minutes, remove the pan from the oven and, using a spatula, rotate the rutabagas to ensure even cooking. Return to the oven.
5. The rutabagas should be soft all the way through and browed on the outside when done. The best way to check for doneness is to pull a piece off the tray, allow it to cool and taste it.

BARLEY WITH FALL VEGETABLES

SERVES 8 AS A SIDE DISH

INGREDIENTS
1 cup pearl barley, rinsed and drained
2 cups water
½ teaspoon coarse Sea Salt
½ lb. bacon (optional)
2 shallots, sliced
1 cup rutabagas, diced and roasted as explained in previous recipe
1 cup carrots, diced and roasted (page 92)
1 cup butternut squash, diced and roasted (page 93)
1 cup Brussels sprouts leaves, roasted (page 110)

Bring 2 cups of water and salt to boil in a medium sauce-pan. Mix in barley. Cover pan, reduce heat to medium and simmer until barley is tender, about 30 minutes. Drain barley.

Cook the bacon either in a pan on the stove top or on a sheet pan in a 350 degree oven for about 20 minutes. After bacon is crisp, place on paper towels to absorb excess fat. When cool, break into small pieces and set aside.

In a sauté pan, heat 3 tablespoons of Olive Oil along with the shallots. Cook for 1 minute and then add the cooked barley. Toss and remove from heat. Combine with roasted root vegetables, Brussels sprouts and bacon. Makes an excellent side dish for roasted chicken (page 119). This can also be served cold, dressed with Maple Cider Vinaigrette (page 178).

ZUCCHINI

INGREDIENTS
2 each zucchini or yellow squash
Olive Oil, Sea Salt & Pepper
3 – 5 fresh mint leaves

TO PREP
Wash the squash, cut off the top and bottom and discard. Slice into uniform round disks about ¼ inch thick. For baby squash, cut in half or quarters lengthwise.

METHOD
1. Preheat the oven to 375 degrees.
2. Have the squash prepped and cut as described above.
3. Place the rounds in a bowl, then toss to coat with Olive Oil, Sea Salt & Pepper.
4. Place on a sheet pan with sides and roast in the oven for about 15 – 25 minutes.
5. The squash should be a little browned on the outside and soft on the inside when done.
6. Top with chopped fresh mint and serve.

TIP
* This is also great topped with roasted cherry tomatoes (page 107) and fresh basil instead of the mint.

CARROTS & PARSNIPS

INGREDIENTS
5 carrots
5 parsnips
Olive Oil, Sea Salt & Pepper

TO PREP
Peel the carrots and parsnips and cut in half lengthwise. Cut into quarters lengthwise for thicker pieces.

METHOD
1. Preheat the oven to 375 degrees.
2. Have the carrots and parsnips prepped and cut uniformly as described above.
3. Place them on a sheet pan with sides and drizzle with Olive Oil, Sea Salt & Pepper. Use your hands to move them around on the pan to coat evenly.
4. Roast in the oven for 12 – 15 minutes. After 10 minutes, remove the pan from the oven and, using a spatula, rotate the carrots to ensure even cooking. Return to the oven.
5. The carrots and parsnips should be soft all the way through and slightly browned when done.

TIP
* Serve as a side dish along with roasted Brussels sprouts. This is a great Thanksgiving side dish.

BUTTERNUT SQUASH

INGREDIENTS

1 butternut squash (about 1 ½ lbs.)
Olive Oil, Sea Salt & Pepper

TO PREP

Cut off top and bottom of the squash, then cut in half where the neck ends and the round bottom begins. Remove the outer skin with a peeler or a knife and scoop out the inside of the round end with a spoon. Dice the squash into uniform pieces to ensure even cooking.

METHOD

1. Preheat the oven to 375 degrees.
2. Have the butternut squash prepped and cut uniformly, as described above.
3. Place the butternut squash in a bowl, then toss and coat with Olive Oil (2 – 3 tablespoons), Sea Salt & Pepper.
4. Place on a sheet pan and roast in the oven for 20 – 25 minutes. After 15 minutes, remove the pan from the oven and, using a spatula, rotate the squash to ensure even cooking. Return to the oven.
5. The squash should be soft all the way through and browned when done.

ROASTED BUTTERNUT SQUASH & RED LEAF SALAD

SERVES 2

INGREDIENTS

1 cup roasted butternut squash (roasted as explained in previous recipe)
3 oz. red leaf lettuce, washed and spun dry
¼ cup pecan halves, toasted
¼ cup dried cranberries
½ cup shaved ricotta salata (shave with a peeler)
Maple-Cider Vinaigrette (page 178)
Sea Salt & Pepper to taste

Heat the oven to 350 degrees. Place the pecans on a sheet pan and drizzle with about 1 teaspoon of Olive Oil and a touch of Sea Salt and toss to coat. Toast in the oven for 5 – 8 minutes. Remove from the oven and allow to cool. Prepare the Maple Cider Vinaigrette as seen on page 178. In a large bowl, combine the butternut squash, lettuce, pecans and cranberries. Add enough vinaigrette to coat the greens and season with Sea Salt & Pepper. Toss gently and top with shaved ricotta salata.

MUSHROOMS

INGREDIENTS
2 portabella mushroom caps
Olive Oil, Sea Salt & Pepper

TO PREP
Remove stems if needed and brush off any dirt from the caps using a paper towel.

METHOD
1. Preheat the oven to 375 degrees.
2. Have the mushrooms prepped as described above.
3. Place on a sheet pan, drizzle with Olive Oil, Sea Salt & Pepper and roast in the oven for about 10 minutes.
4. The mushrooms should be soft all the way through when done. The best way to check is to stick the caps with a knife. If it goes in and comes out easily, they are done.

TIPS
* These meaty mushrooms can work as a main dish and pair well with fall and winter vegetables, such as spinach, winter greens, butternut squash and sweet potatoes.
* All varieties of mushrooms can be roasted as well. Make sure they are all cut into uniform pieces and follow the same method as described above.

PORTABELLAS ALSO MAKE GREAT BURGERS
Top a bun with the roasted portabella, avocado, tomato, red onion, edamame, hummus and arugula. Or, top the portabella with Swiss cheese, caramelized onions, roasted red peppers and a little Dijon mustard. Serve with a side of sweet potato fries (page 96). Create a gluten free sandwich by making the mushroom the bun. Stuff with roasted red pepper, roasted asparagus and soft goat cheese.

ROASTED SHITAKE & TALEGGIO CROSTINI

SERVES 6 AS AN APPETIZER

INGREDIENTS
½ baguette, cut into ¼ inch thick slices
5 oz. taleggio cheese, outer rind removed, sliced
5 oz. shitake mushrooms, stems removed and roasted as explained in previous recipe
2 sprigs fresh thyme
Extra virgin Olive Oil
Sea Salt & Pepper to taste

Preheat oven to 375 degrees. On a sheet pan, lay the shitakes top-side down, drizzle with Olive Oil, Sea Salt & Pepper and roast for about 6 minutes. Place sliced baguette on a sheet pan and brush or drizzle with Olive Oil & Sea Salt. Place in the oven for 6 – 8 minutes or until toasted. Remove from the oven and top with slices of taleggio cheese and roasted shitake caps. Place back in the oven for 1 minute to melt the cheese and serve.

TIP
* Delicious! They can be eaten as a meal with a mixed green salad or served as an appetizer.

SWEET POTATOES

INGREDIENTS
2 sweet potatoes
Olive Oil, Sea Salt & Pepper

TO PREP
Wash the sweet potatoes well. Cut into uniform wedges lengthwise.

METHOD
1. Preheat the oven to 375 degrees.
2. Have the sweet potatoes cut as described above.
3. Place the wedges in a bowl, then toss to coat with Olive Oil, Sea Salt & Pepper.
4. Place on a sheet pan spaced out and roast in the oven for about 35 – 40 minutes. Remove the pan from the oven three-fourths of the way through cooking to rotate the pan and the vegetables on the sheet pan for even cooking.
5. The sweet potatoes should be browned and soft on the inside when done.

TIPS
* Serve with roasted kale or as a side with a portabella burger.
* Also excellent with roasted chicken (page 119) and roasted Brussels sprouts (page 110)

These sweet potato "fries" are an ideal side dish for kids and adults, and have numerous health benefits. Sometimes I just make sweet potato fries and roasted broccoli for dinner and call it a night!

KALE

INGREDIENTS
1 bunch kale
Olive Oil, Sea Salt & Pepper

TO PREP
Cut away any inner ribs and stems and discard. Tear apart into large pieces. Wash the kale well and dry in a salad spinner.

METHOD
1. Preheat the oven to 350 degrees.
2. Have the kale prepped as shown above.
3. Toss in a bowl to coat with Olive Oil, Sea Salt & Pepper.
4. Arrange on a sheet pan in one even layer and roast in the oven for 15 minutes. After 10 minutes, remove from the oven and rotate the kale and the pan to ensure even cooking, then return to the oven.
5. The kale should be crunchy when done.

TIP
* These roasted kale chips, served along with sweet potato fries (at left), make for a power-packed snack.

BROCCOLI

INGREDIENTS
1 lb. broccoli
Olive Oil, Sea Salt & Pepper

TO PREP
Using a paring knife, first cut the florets off the top of the broccoli, then cut down into smaller, uniform sized pieces. Remove the tough outer skin from the stalk and slice the peeled stalk crosswise into small disks.

METHOD
1. Preheat the oven to 375 degrees.
2. Have the broccoli prepped and cut uniformly, as described above.
3. Place the broccoli in a bowl, then toss to coat with Olive Oil, Sea Salt & Pepper.
4. Place on a sheet pan and roast in the oven for about 10 – 15 minutes. After 8 minutes, remove the pan from the oven and, using a spatula, rotate the broccoli to ensure even cooking. Then return to the oven.
5. If you are able to pierce the broccoli easily with a knife, it is ready. When the broccoli is done, it should be a little browned on the outside, pliable, but with a slight crunch.

TIPS
* Add whole garlic cloves at Step 3 to roast along with the broccoli if you like.
* Add red pepper flakes after roasting for a little kick!
* A bowl of this broccoli on its own is delicious. It also goes great with roasted sweet potatoes (page 96) and is a perfect side for roasted chicken (page 119).

This is such a quick, easy and delicious way to prepare broccoli. I actually caught myself telling my son to "stop eating all the broccoli off the pan so there will be enough for everyone else."

CAULIFLOWER

INGREDIENTS
1 head cauliflower
Olive Oil, Sea Salt & Pepper

TO PREP
Remove the core from the bottom of the cauliflower along with the outer leaves. Cut the individual florets off of the main stem using a small paring knife. Discard the stem and cut the florets into even sizes.

METHOD
1. Preheat the oven to 375 degrees.
2. Have the cauliflower prepped and cut uniformly as described above.
3. Place the cauliflower in a bowl, then toss to coat with Olive Oil, Sea Salt & Pepper.
4. Place the cauliflower on a sheet pan and roast in the oven for about 12 – 15 minutes. After 10 minutes, remove the pan from the oven and, using a spatula, rotate the cauliflower to ensure even cooking. Then return to the oven.
5. When the cauliflower is done, it should be a little browned on the outside and tender on the inside.

TIPS
* After roasting, add ¼ cup of toasted pine nuts and ¼ cup of golden raisins for an excellent side dish.

ASPARAGUS

INGREDIENTS
1 lb. asparagus
Olive Oil, Sea Salt & Pepper

TO PREP
Cut 2 – 3 inches off the bottom of the asparagus. There is typically a natural breaking point between the top two-thirds of the asparagus and the woody bottom.

METHOD
1. Preheat the oven to 375 degrees.
2. Have the asparagus prepped as described above.
3. Place the asparagus on a sheet pan with sides, then drizzle with Olive Oil, Sea Salt & Pepper. Use your hands to move the asparagus around on the pan to coat evenly.
4. Roast in the oven for 12 – 15 minutes. Rotate the asparagus two-thirds of the way through the roasting time to ensure even cooking.
5. The asparagus should be soft, pliable and slightly browned when done.

TIPS
* This quick and easy side dish is ideal for serving large groups when you have limited time or to accompany a piece of fish or meat for one.
* Use roasted asparagus in a warm panini with sun dried tomatoes and soft goat cheese.

COUSCOUS WITH ROASTED ASPARAGUS, FENNEL & SHITAKES

SERVES 6

INGREDIENTS
1 cup couscous
1 ½ cups water
¼ teaspoon Sea Salt
3 tablespoons extra virgin Olive Oil
1 teaspoon garlic, minced
1 bunch asparagus, roasted as explained in previous recipe and cut crosswise into ½ inch pieces
1 bulb fennel, roasted (page 88) and diced
6 oz. shitake mushrooms, stems removed and tops cut into thin strips
2 tablespoons parsley, chopped

Cook couscous in salted water as instructed. In a large sauté pan warm 3 tablespoons of Olive Oil and 1 teaspoon of minced garlic. Add the shitakes, season with Sea Salt & Pepper and cook for 1 – 2 minutes. Add the cooked couscous. Remove from heat and combine with fennel, asparagus and parsley. Drizzle with extra virgin Olive Oil and season with Sea Salt & Pepper if needed. Enjoy warm or cold.

EGGPLANT

INGREDIENTS
2 eggplant
Olive Oil, Sea Salt & Pepper

TO PREP
Wash the eggplant, cut off the top and discard. Cut lengthwise into uniform ¼ inch slices.

METHOD
1. Preheat the oven to 400 degrees.
2. Have the eggplant cut as described above.
3. Place the sliced eggplant in a bowl, then toss to coat with Olive Oil, Sea Salt & Pepper.
4. Place on a sheet pan spaced out and roast in the oven for about 15 minutes. Rotate the pan halfway through roasting for even cooking.
5. The eggplant should be a little browned and soft on the inside when done.

TIPS
* If serving a group, cut the cooked eggplant pieces on an angle into 4 or 5 smaller pieces.
* Use this roasted eggplant to make eggplant parmesan, instead of the typical fried method.

EGGPLANT PARMESAN

SERVES 8

INGREDIENTS
4 – 5 large eggplant, sliced and roasted as explained in previous recipe
4 ½ cups Fresh Tomato Sauce (page 50)
¾ cup grated parmesan
2 cups fresh mozzarella, pulled apart or sliced into thin rounds
½ cup fresh basil, chopped
Olive Oil, Sea Salt & Pepper

Preheat oven to 350 degrees. Spread a thin layer (about ¼ cup) of Fresh Tomato Sauce on the bottom of a 9 x 13 inch pan. Layer the eggplant, then the tomato sauce, fresh mozzarella, a sprinkle of parmesan and fresh basil. Repeat the layers three more times for a total of 4 layers. Place the eggplant parmesan in the oven and bake for 30 – 40 minutes or until slightly browned on top. Allow to cool for about 10 – 20 minutes before slicing and serving.

ROMA TOMATOES

INGREDIENTS

12 plum tomatoes (Roma)
Olive Oil, Sea Salt & Pepper

TO PREP

Wash the Roma tomatoes and cut the tops off, then cut in half lengthwise.

METHOD

1. Preheat the oven to 180 degrees.
2. Place the cut tomatoes in a bowl, then toss and coat with Olive Oil, Sea Salt & Pepper.
3. Place seed side up on a sheet pan and roast in the oven for 6 – 7 hours.
4. The tomatoes will shrink down to what looks like a plumper sun dried tomato. They should still contain some moisture. The flavors will be condensed, resulting in a very flavorful tomato.

TIPS

* These tomatoes are wonderful on sandwiches, in pasta dishes and in salads. I personally like them on top of my favorite bread on their own or with a fresh ricotta or soft goat cheese, then drizzled with extra virgin Olive Oil.
* Give the tomatoes an upscale treatment by serving them as a sandwich on focaccia with lobster and arugula.
* Oven roasted roma tomatoes also make an excellent salad dressing (page 179).

BRUSCHETTA

SERVES 10 AS AN APPETIZER

INGREDIENTS

10 plum tomatoes, roasted as explained in previous recipe
1 baguette, sliced
1 cup fresh ricotta or soft goat cheese
Extra virgin Olive Oil, Sea Salt & Pepper

Slice the baguette on the bias into ¼ inch slices. Brush both sides of the bread with extra virgin Olive Oil and toast on a sheet pan in a 350 degree oven for 8 – 10 minutes or until golden brown. Spread ricotta cheese on each slice, drizzle with extra virgin Olive Oil and season with Sea Salt & Pepper. Top with tomatoes.

CHERRY TOMATOES

INGREDIENTS
1 pint cherry tomatoes
Olive Oil, Sea Salt & Pepper

TO PREP
Wash and dry cherry tomatoes and remove stems.

METHOD
1. Preheat the oven to 375 degrees.
2. Place the tomatoes in a bowl, then toss and coat with Olive Oil, Sea Salt & Pepper.
3. Place on a sheet pan and roast in the oven for 10 – 15 minutes. The tomatoes will blister and lightly brown.
4. Top with fresh basil.

TIPS
* These oven roasted cherry tomatoes accompany sautéed halibut (page 67) beautifully and also go well with sautéed spinach (page 55).
* Add capers and kalamata olives if desired. Drizzle with good extra virgin Olive Oil.
* They also make a great pizza topping instead of using a traditional tomato sauce.

MEDITERRANEAN PIZZA

SERVES 3 – 4

INGREDIENTS
Premade pizza dough
2 pints cherry or grape tomatoes, roasted as explained in previous recipe
2 teaspoons garlic, minced
2 – 3 tablespoons extra virgin Olive Oil
2 tablespoons capers
¼ cup kalamata olives, pitted and halved
1 cup mozzarella cheese, shredded

Preheat oven to 375 degrees. Carefully stretch the dough out into an even thin round on a pizza pan sprayed with Olive Oil. Combine the minced garlic with 2 tablespoons of extra virgin Olive Oil and spread evenly over the dough using the back of a large spoon. Top evenly with the roasted cherry tomatoes, capers and olives. Top with mozzarella cheese and place in the oven for 10 – 12 minutes. About 8 minutes into cooking, slide the pizza off the pan and directly onto the oven rack so the bottom can crisp for 2 – 4 additional minutes. Using tongs, slide the pizza back onto the pan, then transfer to a rack to cool. Wait 5 minutes before cutting. Slice and serve.

SPAGHETTI SQUASH

INGREDIENTS
1 spaghetti squash
Olive Oil, Sea Salt & Pepper

TO PREP
Cut the squash in half lengthwise. Scoop the seeds out with a spoon and discard.

METHOD
1. Preheat the oven to 375 degrees.
2. Have the spaghetti squash prepped, cut in half and seeded as described above.
3. Drizzle the inside of the squash with Olive Oil, Sea Salt & Pepper.
4. Wrap squash halves together face up in tin foil, place on a sheet pan and roast in the oven for up to 2 hours.
5. The squash should be soft all the way through when done. The best way to check is with a paring knife. You should be able to slide the knife in and out easily.
6. Allow to cool. Then, using a fork, scrape away the inside from the skin. It should easily break into spaghetti-like pieces.
7. Drizzle with good quality extra virgin Olive Oil, Sea Salt & Pepper. You can also sauté it with minced garlic, or prepare as described below.

TIP
* My favorite way to prepare spaghetti squash is the same way I would prepare spaghetti. In fact, when my kids were young and addicted to all things pasta, I would replace the pasta with squash. They never knew the difference!

SPAGHETTI SQUASH WITH FRESH TOMATOES & BASIL

SERVES 4

INGREDIENTS
1 small spaghetti squash, prepared as explained in previous recipe and scooped out of the skin
2 cloves garlic, sliced thin
6 roma tomatoes, diced
5 leaves fresh basil, cut into strips
Extra virgin Olive Oil
Sea Salt & Pepper

Place the garlic in a sauté pan with 3 tablespoons of Olive Oil on medium-low heat. Allow garlic to become fragrant (1 minute), then, before it browns, add the tomatoes. Season with Sea Salt & Pepper. Turn the heat up to medium and allow the tomatoes to break down and cook for an additional 10 minutes. Add the squash to the tomatoes, combine well and remove from the heat. Add fresh basil and season again with Sea Salt & Pepper. Finish with a drizzle of extra virgin Olive Oil.

HOW TO ROAST:
BRUSSELS SPROUTS

INGREDIENTS
1 lb. Brussels sprouts
5 whole garlic cloves
Olive Oil, Sea Salt & Pepper

TO PREP
Cut off the bottom stem of the Brussels
sprouts and remove the outer leaves. Using
a paring knife, remove the core and cut in
half, lengthwise.

METHOD
1. Preheat the oven to 350 degrees.
2. Have the Brussels sprouts prepped as
described above.
3. Place them in a bowl along with 5 garlic
cloves, then toss and coat with Olive Oil, Sea
Salt & Pepper.
4. Place on a sheet pan with sides and roast
in the oven for about 15 minutes. After 10 minutes, remove the pan from the oven and, using
a spatula, rotate the Brussels sprouts to ensure
even cooking. Return to the oven.
5. The Brussels sprouts should be slightly
browned and the garlic should be soft and
slightly browned.

TIPS
* You cannot go wrong serving these roasted
Brussels sprouts beside any piece of meat
or fish, such as roasted chicken (page 119),
sautéed salmon (page 64), halibut (page 67) or
steak (page 76).
* Combine with other roasted vegetables in
this section for additional sides.

WHOLE FISH

INGREDIENTS

**1 to 2½ lb. red snapper or striped bass,
gutted, with scales and gills removed
(serves 3)**
1 lemon
3 sprigs fresh thyme
1 cup white wine
Olive Oil, Sea Salt & Pepper

TO PREP

Rinse the fish under cold water and dry well on paper
towels. Make three diagonal slits about ½ inch deep in
the skin on both sides.

METHOD

1. Preheat your oven to 400 degrees.
2. Coat the fish well with Olive Oil, Sea Salt & Pepper.
3. Lay the fish on a sheet pan with aluminum foil under-
neath pulled up slightly on the ends.
4. Place 3 slices of lemon and thyme inside the cavity of
the fish and pour white wine over it.
5. Place the fish in the oven for about 30 minutes or
until the flesh flakes easily when lightly pressed. The
fish will continue to carry-over cook after you remove
it from the oven.
6. Allow fish to rest for 5 – 10 minutes before serving.
Use a fork to remove the skin and a spatula to remove
the fillets from the bone.

Drizzle generously with good, cold pressed extra virgin
Olive Oil, squeeze fresh lemon juice over top and season
with Sea Salt & Pepper as needed.

TIP

* Roasted asparagus (page 101) is an easy side dish to
serve with this fish.

SALMON

INGREDIENTS
1 lb. salmon
Olive Oil, Sea Salt & Pepper

TO PREP
Remove the skin, rinse the fish under cold water and dry well on paper towels.

METHOD
1. Preheat the oven to 375 degrees.
2. Coat the fish well with Olive Oil, Sea Salt & Pepper.
3. Lay the fish on a sheet pan and place it in the oven for 8 – 12 minutes or until the flesh flakes easily when lightly pressed. Salmon should be served medium-rare to medium. The fish will continue to carry-over cook after you remove it from the oven.
4. Allow fish to rest for 5 minutes before serving. Drizzle generously with good, cold pressed extra virgin Olive Oil and squeeze fresh lemon juice over top if desired.

SALMON & LENTILS

SERVES 5

INGREDIENTS
2 lbs. salmon, prepared as in previous recipe
1 cup French green lentils
3 cups water
1 teaspoon garlic, minced
¼ cup onion, small diced
¼ cup fennel, small diced
¼ cup carrot, small diced
¼ cup celery, small diced
¼ cup parsley, chopped
Extra virgin Olive Oil as needed
Sea Salt & Pepper to taste

Cook lentils in 3 cups of lightly salted water (about ¾ teaspoon Sea Salt) over low heat until all the water is absorbed. Set aside. In a large sauté pan, warm 2 tablespoons of Olive Oil along with the diced onion and minced garlic. Sauté for 1 minute and then add the fennel. Increase the heat to high, add the carrots and celery and sauté for an additional minute. Season with Sea Salt & Pepper. Add the lentils, remove from the heat and combine with the parsley. Season as needed with Sea Salt & Pepper and drizzle with additional extra virgin Olive Oil. Serve with the salmon.
* Another great addition to this plate is blanched asparagus (page 162).

SHRIMP

INGREDIENTS

1 pound large shrimp, peeled and deveined
Olive Oil, Sea Salt & Pepper

TO PREP

Shrimp can be purchased already peeled and deveined. If not, peel the shrimp, leaving the tails on, and devein by cutting a small incision along the top of the shrimp and removing and discarding the black or clear string. Rinse under cold water and dry well using paper towels.

METHOD

1. Preheat the oven to 375 degrees.
2. On a sheet pan with sides, lay the shrimp in a row and drizzle evenly with Olive Oil and season with Sea Salt & Pepper.
3. Put the shrimp in the oven for 5 minutes or until cooked through. Be careful not to overcook them. The shrimp should be pink and white all the way through, not opaque. They will continue to carry-over cook after you remove them from the oven.

TIP

* If you have fresh thyme or rosemary on hand, you can lay the shrimp on top of the herb sprigs while roasting.

OVEN ROASTED SHRIMP WITH LEMON & BASIL ORZO

SERVES 2

INGREDIENTS

1 pound medium shrimp, peeled (tails off), deveined and roasted as explained in previous recipe
½ lb. orzo
5 tablespoons good extra virgin Olive Oil
½ teaspoon garlic, minced
¾ cup scallion, both green and white parts, thinly sliced
½ cup red onion, finely diced
2 tablespoons capers
2 tablespoons basil, cut into thin strips
2 tablespoons fresh lemon juice

Prepare the shrimp as previous recipe explains. Cook the orzo in boiling salted water according to the instructions. Drain, set aside and allow to cool. Warm 3 tablespoons of Olive Oil in a large sauté pan. Add the garlic, onions and scallions and cook until fragrant, about 1 minute. Remove from heat and stir in the orzo, lemon juice, the additional 2 tablespoons of extra virgin Olive Oil and season with Sea Salt & Pepper. Add shrimp and basil. Eat immediately or refrigerate and enjoy cold.

ROASTED CHICKEN

INGREDIENTS
1 chicken 3 ½ – 4 lbs.
½ lemon
2 sprigs rosemary
2 cloves garlic
Olive Oil, Sea Salt & Pepper

TO PREP
Rinse the chicken under cold water. Remove all innards or bag from the inside cavity and discard. Place the chicken on paper towels to dry.

METHOD
1. Preheat oven to 375.
2. Have the chicken prepped as described above.
3. Fill the cavity with the lemon, rosemary and garlic.
4. Truss the chicken by tying the legs together with butcher's twine.
5. Place the trussed, stuffed bird in a bowl, drizzle with Olive Oil and season well with coarse Sea Salt & Pepper. Rotate in the bowl to coat evenly. Place the chicken onto a rack that fits onto a sheet pan or roasting pan. Aluminum foil can be put on the sheet pan under the rack for easier cleanup, but it is not necessary.
6. Roast in the oven for 60 – 75 minutes. Check the chicken for doneness by cutting the skin between the breast and the leg. The juices that sit between the two should be clear. If you see any redness or blood, return chicken to the oven until the juices run clear. Remove from the oven and allow to rest for 20 minutes before serving or for an hour before pulling apart.
7. Once the chicken has completely cooled, you can begin to remove the meat from the bone. Remove and discard all skin and bones. Break the meat into small pieces onto the bottom of the roasting pan. Allow the meat to soak up all the juices at the bottom of the pan and then place in a container and store in the refrigerator for later use.

TIP
* This roasted chicken is great to keep on hand for sandwiches or for adding to salads throughout the week. It may be worth it to roast two chickens at a time, one to eat immediately and one to pull apart to add to salad, tacos, sandwiches or quesadillas as shown on the following page.

CHICKEN QUESADILLA

SERVES 4

INGREDIENTS
4 flour tortillas
1 cup shredded cheddar cheese or use
pepper jack if you like a little kick
1 cup roasted chicken (page 119)

Lay the flour tortillas flat and lightly sprinkle with
cheese. Place the pulled pieces of chicken on one half
of each of the tortillas. Be sure not to over-stuff the
tortillas with cheese or chicken. A little bit goes a long
way. Place a non-stick sauté pan, large enough for the
size of the tortilla, on medium-low heat. Coat the bottom of the pan evenly with a non-stick spray or Olive
Oil, then carefully place the tortilla in the pan. Cook
for about 3 minutes or until cheese is melted and the
tortilla is slightly browned and crisp. Using a spatula,
fold in half, remove from the pan and place on a cutting
board. The quesadilla slices easier after it has cooled for
a minute. Serve with guacamole and a salad.

EASY GUACAMOLE

SERVES 4

INGREDIENTS
2 ripe avocados
1 lime
Sea Salt

Cut the avocado in half lengthwise and remove the large
seed. Using a small paring knife, make cuts lengthwise
and crosswise into the avocado while still in its skin.
Using a spoon, scoop out the avocado into a bowl. Squeeze
the lime over the avocado and mix well, continuing to
mash with the spoon. Season to taste with Sea Salt.
Serve as an accompaniment to the quesadilla.

BEEF TENDERLOIN

INGREDIENTS

4 – 5 lb. whole beef tenderloin, trimmed (serves 10)
3 – 4 sprigs fresh rosemary
Olive Oil, Sea Salt & Pepper

TO PREP

Trim off any excess fat from the tenderloin and dry on paper towels if needed.

METHOD

1. Preheat oven to 375 degrees.
2. Have the tenderloin trimmed and dry.
3. Season well on all sides with Sea Salt & Pepper.
4. Heat a large sauté pan on high.
5. Add a small amount of Olive Oil.
6. Place the tenderloin in the pan and allow to brown for 2 – 3 minutes on each side.
7. Transfer the tenderloin to a sheet pan (unless the whole sauté pan can fit in your oven) with rosemary sprigs under the meat and place in the oven for about 18 – 20 minutes or until cooked to your liking.
8. Remove from the oven and allow the meat to rest for 20 minutes. It will continue to cook and the juices will distribute within the meat. If the tenderloin is sliced before it rests, all of the juices will run out, resulting in dry meat.
9. Slice and finish with good extra virgin Olive Oil before serving.

TIPS

* Cooking temperatures (using a thermometer):
rare 120 – 125 degrees, medium-rare 130 – 135 degrees, medium 140 – 145 degrees, medium-well 150 – 155 degrees, well done 160 degrees and above.
* If you slice the meat (once) after it rests and want it more cooked, place it back in the oven at 350 degrees for 5 minutes or until it is cooked to your liking.
* Cooking time will vary depending on the thickness of the cut.
* This beef tenderloin goes well with any vegetable in the Grill or Roast sections.

I typically use beef tenderloin when I am entertaining large groups. I cook it as shown above the day before the event, allow it to cool and keep it in the refrigerator overnight. The next day, I slice it thin using a serrated knife and display it along with small rolls, arugula and a horseradish sauce for guests to make sandwiches or I serve it with grilled vegetables (also cooked in advance and served cold) and a salad.

HORSERADISH SAUCE

SERVES 10

INGREDIENTS

¾ cup sour cream
½ cup mayonnaise
⅓ cup Dijon mustard
2 tablespoons grain mustard
3 tablespoons horseradish cream (this can be found in the same aisle as mustard and mayonnaise at your local grocery store)

Combine all 5 ingredients in a bowl. Can be made up to a week in advance.

GRILL

Whether you prefer gas or charcoal, this method provides fast, easy cooking with little cleanup. Grilling is the way to go if you are short on time and have a large group to feed. Grilling can also be done hours in advance. Serve the food at room temperature or flash it in the oven to reheat.

GRILL NOTES

* If your vegetables are burning instead of grilling, lower the heat and cover the grill until the flames die down.

* It is easier to grill vegetables in large pieces and cut them into smaller bites after grilling.

* Remember, the cooking times in this section are "suggested times." Because of the variation in types and temperatures of grills, the times listed should be used as a general guide only.

* Every recipe in this section calls for getting the grill "Hot." This is to heat the grate, which will prevent sticking and make beautiful grill marks. After the grate gets hot you can adjust the heat appropriately.

BEETS

INGREDIENTS

**1 bunch beets, red or gold, 3 per bunch
(this will yield enough for 4 portions)
Olive Oil, Sea Salt & Pepper**

TO PREP

Cut off the tops and tails of the beets. If the greens are in good shape, they can be washed and sautéed (page 55). Wash and scrub the beets to remove dirt.

METHOD

1. Prepare the beets as described above. Peel the skin and slice them into uniform rounds, about ¼ inch thick.
2. Get the grill HOT.
3. Drizzle beets with Olive Oil, Sea Salt & Pepper. Toss to coat evenly.
4. Grill on medium heat for about 5 – 8 minutes on each side or until cooked through.
5. Finish with good extra virgin Olive Oil before serving.

TIPS

* You may want to use plastic gloves to avoid red stained hands.
* Baby beets can also be grilled. Just scrub to remove dirt, halve or quarter them and follow the same method as above.
* Cover or close the grill while cooking. It is better to cook beets longer on lower heat to ensure they cook thoroughly.

GRILLED BEET & ASPARAGUS SALAD WITH CRUMBLED GOAT CHEESE

SERVES 4

INGREDIENTS

**3 beets (one bunch), grilled as explained in previous recipe
1 pound asparagus (one bunch), grilled (page 133)
½ cup goat cheese, crumbled
Extra virgin Olive Oil (as needed)
Sea Salt & Pepper
Saba (optional) [Saba is cooked grape must. It is sweet and similar to reduced balsamic vinegar and is sold at specialty stores such as Williams-Sonoma.]**

Grill beets and asparagus. Divide the beets and asparagus evenly among 4 plates. Sprinkle with crumbled goat cheese and drizzle with extra virgin Olive Oil (and saba if desired). Season with Sea Salt & Pepper as needed.

BELL PEPPERS, EGGPLANT
& FENNEL

SERVES 4

INGREDIENTS
**2 red bell peppers, cut in four pieces each,
centers, stems and seeds discarded
1 eggplant, cut lengthwise into ½ inch
pieces
1 fennel bulb, quartered
Olive Oil, Sea Salt & Pepper**

Prepare the vegetables as described above. Get the grill
HOT (this will prevent sticking). Drizzle with Olive Oil,
Sea Salt & Pepper. Toss to coat evenly. Grill 2 – 4 minutes
on each side or until cooked through. Finish with good
extra virgin Olive Oil before serving.

TIPS
* If you find that the vegetables are burning or browning
too quickly, cover the grill and lower the heat if you are
working with a gas grill.
* Serve with a mixed green salad or along with any other
grilled vegetables, meat or fish in this section.

ONIONS, LEEKS & SCALLIONS

SERVES 4

INGREDIENTS

1 large onion, red or sweet, peeled and cut into ½ inch disks
2 leeks, washed well and cut in half, leaving the stems intact
1 bunch scallions, trimmed and washed
Olive Oil, Sea Salt & Pepper

Prepare the vegetables as described above. Set the grill to a medium heat. Drizzle with Olive Oil, Sea Salt & Pepper. Toss or brush vegetables to coat evenly. Grill scallions 1 minute per side (uncovered). Grill onions and leeks 5 – 8 minutes per side, keeping grill covered while cooking. Finish with good quality extra virgin Olive Oil and serve.

TIPS

* Grill these onions on a lower heat. The longer they cook the more sugars are released and the sweeter they get. Because onions do contain sugar they caramelize fast and burn easily on high heat.
* This grilled threesome is an excellent accompaniment to other grilled vegetables, grilled steak or fish.

ZUCCHINI

INGREDIENTS
2 zucchini and/or yellow squash
Olive Oil, Sea Salt & Pepper

TO PREP
Cut off the top and bottom of the squash. Then cut lengthwise into ¼ inch thick pieces using a knife or mandolin. For baby squash, cut in half lengthwise. It is much easier to grill in large long slices rather than small circles.

METHOD
1. Prepare the zucchini and/or yellow squash as explained above.
2. Get your grill HOT (this will prevent sticking).
3. Place squash on a sheet pan, drizzle with Olive Oil, Sea Salt & Pepper.
4. Toss to coat evenly.
5. Grill 1 – 3 minutes on each side or until cooked through.
6. After the zucchini is grilled it can be served whole or cut on the bias into smaller 2 inch pieces.

TIP
* Top with a chiffonade (a cooking technique in which the herbs are cut into long thin strips) of fresh mint and serve as a side with grilled scallops, halibut or lamb.

GRILLED ZUCCHINI & GOAT CHEESE ROLLS

MAKES ABOUT 20 BITE-SIZE ROLLS

INGREDIENTS
2 zucchini about 9 inches long, or 4 small zucchini, cut and grilled as explained in previous recipe
3 oz. goat cheese
2 basil leaves, chiffonade (thinly sliced)
2 tablespoons pine nuts, toasted (page 83) (optional)
¼ teaspoon lemon zest, minced
1 tablespoon extra virgin Olive Oil,
Sea Salt & Pepper
20 Toothpicks

Grill the zucchini as explained and lay the strips side by side on a sheet pan to cool. Cut the zucchini in half when cooled. In a small bowl, mix together the goat cheese, basil, toasted pine nuts, lemon zest and extra virgin Olive Oil. Season with Sea Salt & Pepper. Divide the goat cheese mixture evenly in small balls at the end of each zucchini strip, then roll up. Serve as finger food or use a toothpick to hold. Works great as an hors d'oeuvre.

ASPARAGUS

INGREDIENTS
1 lb. asparagus
Olive Oil, Sea Salt & Pepper

TO PREP
Cut $^1/_3$ off the bottom of the asparagus bunch. There is typically a natural breaking point between the top two-thirds of the asparagus and the woody bottom.

METHOD
1. Prepare the asparagus as explained above.
2. Get the grill HOT.
3. Drizzle the asparagus with Olive Oil, Sea Salt & Pepper.
4. Toss to coat evenly.
5. Grill 3 – 5 minutes on each side, turning and rotating until cooked through. The thickness of the asparagus will determine the cooking time.

TIP
* Asparagus should be flexible and have some color when done. You can always pull one off the grill and taste it to test for doneness.

LEMON QUINOA WITH GRILLED ASPARAGUS & OLIVES

SERVES 4

INGREDIENTS
1 cup quinoa
2 cups water
1 cup asparagus, grilled and cut into 1 inch pieces
½ cup kalamata olives, cut in half
½ teaspoon lemon zest
2 tablespoons parsley, chopped
2 tablespoons extra virgin Olive Oil
Sea Salt & Pepper

Place the quinoa and water in a saucepan and bring to a boil, then lower to a simmer. Cook for 10 – 15 minutes or until all of the liquid is absorbed. Remove from heat and allow to cool. Add Olive Oil and season with Sea Salt & Pepper. Combine quinoa with all remaining ingredients. Store in the refrigerator and enjoy cold.

HOW TO GRILL:
CARROTS, SWEET POTATO & BUTTERNUT SQUASH

SERVES 4

INGREDIENTS

 6 carrots, peeled and cut in half
 1 sweet potato, cut into ½ inch thick disks
 1 butternut squash, peeled, seeds removed
 from the bottom and sliced into ½ inch
 thick disks
 Olive Oil, Sea Salt & Pepper

Prepare the vegetables as described above. Get the grill HOT (this will prevent sticking). Drizzle the vegetables above with Olive Oil, Sea Salt & Pepper. Toss to coat evenly. Lower grill to medium heat and grill vegetables about 3 minutes on each side or until cooked through.

TIPS

* If you find that the vegetables are burning or browning too quickly, cover the grill and lower the heat if you are working with a gas grill.
* Serve with Manchego Cheese, Dried Cherry & Pecan Salad (page 73) or along with any other grilled vegetables, meat or fish in this section.

CORN

INGREDIENTS

2 ears of fresh corn on the cob, silver queen or bi-colored
Olive Oil, Sea Salt & Pepper

TO PREP

Shuck the corn and wash to remove all silk.

METHOD

1. Prepare the corn as shown above.
2. Get the grill HOT (this will prevent sticking).
3. Drizzle the corn with Olive Oil, Sea Salt & Pepper.
4. Rub or brush to coat the corn evenly.
5. Grill 3 minutes on each side or until you see some grill marks and color.
6. Finish with good quality extra virgin Olive Oil and additional Sea Salt & Pepper if needed.

TIP

* After grilling, corn can be eaten on the cob, or you can cut the kernels off the cob and add to a salad.

GRILLED CORN, TOMATO & BASIL SALAD

SERVES 2

INGREDIENTS

1 ear corn, grilled and cut off the cob
1 large heirloom tomato, diced
2 basil leaves, sliced into strips
2 teaspoons balsamic vinegar
2 tablespoons extra virgin Olive Oil
Sea Salt & Pepper

Combine all ingredients together in a bowl. Season with Sea Salt & Pepper and enjoy!

GRILLED CORN WITH EDAMAME & BLACK BEANS

SERVES 4 – 6 AS A SIDE DISH

INGREDIENTS

1 small red onion, medium diced
1 red bell pepper, diced
2 scallions, sliced (both white and green parts)
1 15 oz. can black beans, drained and rinsed
1 ½ cups edamame (shelled)
2 ears corn, grilled as explained in previous recipe and cut off the cob
3 tablespoons cilantro, chopped (optional)
Extra virgin Olive Oil
Sea salt & Pepper to taste

Warm a large sauté pan on medium-high heat. Add 2 tablespoons of Olive Oil and the diced red onion and sauté for 1 minute. Add the red pepper and scallions and cook for 1 more minute. Then add the black beans, edamame, corn and cilantro. Combine and season with Sea Salt & Pepper.

* This is an easy high-protein mix that is also very popular with kids. It is a great side dish to serve with fajitas or tacos.

CAULIFLOWER

INGREDIENTS

1 head cauliflower
Olive Oil, Sea Salt & Pepper

TO PREP

Remove outer leaves from the cauliflower. Leave the core intact and cut from the top through the core into ¾ inch slices. This is easiest to cut with a long, serrated bread knife. Some of the smaller pieces that break off can't be grilled. Set those smaller pieces aside to roast separately (page 99).

METHOD

1. Prepare the cauliflower as shown above.
2. Get the grill HOT.
3. Place cauliflower on a sheet pan and drizzle with Olive Oil, Sea Salt & Pepper on both sides.
4. Grill on medium heat for about 3 – 6 minutes on each side or until cooked through. Cover the grill while cooking.
5. Finish with good extra virgin Olive Oil before serving.

TIPS

* You can find a colorful variety of cauliflower at your local farmer's market at certain times during the year. Take advantage of the various colors to create a beautiful side dish.
* I would recommend serving this with fish or scallops.

GRILLED CAULIFLOWER WITH BLACK OLIVE VINAIGRETTE

SERVES 4

INGREDIENTS

2 heads of cauliflower, cut and grilled as explained in previous recipe
½ cup pitted kalamata olives
3 tablespoons fresh lemon juice
½ cup extra virgin Olive Oil

Puree lemon juice, olives and Olive Oil in a blender and set aside. Grill cauliflower and drizzle with olive vinaigrette as needed.

* This also makes an excellent appetizer. Set the smaller grilled pieces on a platter and top with a touch of olive vinaigrette.

SCALLOPS

INGREDIENTS

3 – 4 U/10 size scallops per person
Olive Oil, Sea Salt & Pepper
1 lemon wedge per person

TO PREP

Make sure scallops are dry (place between paper towels if needed) with the small muscle found on the side of each scallop removed.

METHOD

1. Get the grill HOT.
2. Coat scallops evenly with Olive Oil, Sea Salt & Pepper.
3. Grill on high heat about 3 minutes per side or until cooked to your liking.
4. Finish off with a good extra virgin Olive Oil and a squeeze of fresh lemon juice.

TIP

* Serve along with your favorite grilled vegetables from the previous pages. I prefer grilled asparagus (page 133) and a salad to complete the meal.

SHRIMP

INGREDIENTS

Shrimp, large, 4 – 5 per person
Olive Oil, Sea Salt & Pepper
1 lemon

TO PREP

Shrimp can be purchased already peeled and deveined. If not, peel the shrimp, leaving the tails on, and devein by cutting a small incision along the top of the shrimp and removing and discarding the black or clear string. Rinse under cold water and dry well using paper towels.

METHOD

1. Get the grill HOT.
2. Place shrimp on a sheet pan, drizzle with Olive Oil and season with Sea Salt & Pepper.
3. Grill about 2 – 3 minutes on each side.
4. Remove from the grill and drizzle with a good extra virgin Olive Oil and fresh lemon juice to serve.

GRILLED SHRIMP WITH GRILLED VEGETABLE COUSCOUS

SERVES 4

INGREDIENTS

20 shrimp, medium, grilled as explained in previous recipe
1 cup couscous
1 ½ cups water
Sea Salt
½ teaspoon garlic, minced
1 medium zucchini, grilled and diced
1 red pepper, grilled and diced
1 small red onion, grilled and diced
Parsley, chopped

Grill vegetables as described on previous pages. Let cool and dice. Grill shrimp as described above and set aside. Cook couscous in salted water as instructed. In a large sauté pan, warm 3 tablespoons of Olive Oil and ½ teaspoon of minced garlic. Add the cooked couscous, remove from heat and combine with zucchini, peppers, onion and parsley. Season with Sea Salt & Pepper if needed. Serve with grilled shrimp. Enjoy warm or cold.

* Quinoa can be used in place of couscous.
* If you make a bunch of grilled vegetables and have leftovers, dice up whatever you have and add to the couscous above.

SALMON

INGREDIENTS
2 lbs. salmon, skin on
Olive Oil, Sea Salt & Pepper

TO PREP
Trim off any excess fat from the side of the salmon, rinse under cold water and dry well using paper towels.

METHOD
1. Get the grill HOT.
2. Coat salmon evenly with Olive Oil, Sea Salt & Pepper.
3. Grill about 3 minutes on each side or until cooked to your liking.
4. For best results, undercook the salmon, remove from the grill and allow it to rest and slowly carry-over cook for an additional 5 minutes.
5. Serve along with your favorite grilled vegetables from the previous pages and finish the salmon with a drizzle of good extra virgin Olive Oil.

TIP
* Cooking time depends on the thickness of the salmon. I much prefer the thicker cuts that are closer to the head side of the fish rather than the thin tail-end cuts. Thinner cuts are easier to overcook and may require even less cooking time per side.

BARBEQUED SALMON

After grilling the salmon as shown above, simply spread on your favorite barbeque sauce. I prefer a thick sweet-style barbeque sauce. Serve with grilled asparagus or coleslaw and blanched snap peas (page 169). This also works with sautéed salmon (page 64).

COLESLAW

SERVES 10

INGREDIENTS
½ head green cabbage, shredded
¼ head red cabbage, shredded
1 cup carrots, julienned or shredded
3 tablespoons apple cider vinegar
2 tablespoons olive oil
¼ cup sugar
2 tablespoons mayonnaise (optional)
1 tablespoon whole grain mustard
Sea Salt & Pepper to taste

Combine all ingredients together in a bowl. Season well with Sea Salt & Pepper. Can be made up to 2 days in advance.

HALIBUT

INGREDIENTS
Halibut, 6 oz. per person
Olive Oil, Sea Salt & Pepper
1 lemon wedge per person

TO PREP
Rinse halibut under cold water and dry well using paper towels.

METHOD
1. Get the grill HOT.
2. Coat the halibut evenly with Olive Oil, Sea Salt & Pepper.
3. Grill about 3 – 5 minutes on each side (depending on thickness) or until cooked to your liking.
4. Finish the halibut with a drizzle of good extra virgin Olive Oil and a squeeze of lemon.

TIP
* Serve along with your favorite grilled vegetables from the previous pages or use my suggestions below.
Other firm fish, such as striped bass, red snapper and sea bass, can be prepared using this same method. Serve along with sautéed greens and caramelized onions (page 55) and oven roasted cherry tomatoes (page 107).

HALIBUT WITH CHIMICHURRI

SERVES 6

INGREDIENTS
6 5 – 6 ounce halibut steaks (about
1 inch thick), grilled as explained in
previous recipe
$1/3$ cup extra virgin Olive Oil
¼ cup fresh lemon juice
1 tablespoon minced garlic
1 tablespoon minced shallot
¾ teaspoon hot red pepper flakes
¾ cup chopped flat leaf parsley

Whisk together Olive Oil, lemon juice, garlic, shallot, red-pepper flakes and ½ tsp. each of Sea Salt & Pepper until salt has dissolved. Stir in parsley. Let chimichurri stand 20 minutes. Prepare the halibut as described above and top with the chimichurri to serve.

SQUID

INGREDIENTS

1 ½ lbs. cleaned squid
Olive Oil, Sea Salt & Pepper
1 lemon

TO PREP

Rinse squid under cold water, then dry well on paper towels. Remove any flaps from the squid body. Score the squid with a knife by making cross marks in the squid without cutting all the way through. Cut large tentacles in half while smaller ones can be left whole.

METHOD

1. Get the grill HOT.
2. In a bowl, drizzle the squid with Olive Oil and season with Sea Salt & Pepper and toss to coat evenly.
3. Grill about 2 – 3 minutes on each side.
4. Remove from the grill and finish with fresh lemon juice and drizzle with a good extra virgin Olive Oil to serve.

GRILLED SQUID WITH LEMON & OLIVES

SERVES 3

INGREDIENTS

1 ½ pounds squid, grilled as explained in previous recipe
2 tablespoons fresh lemon juice
1 small clove garlic, minced
¼ cup kalamata olives, pitted
2 tablespoons parsley, chopped
3 tablespoons extra virgin Olive Oil
Sea Salt & Pepper to taste

Whisk together lemon juice, oil and garlic until combined. Add squid to the dressing and coat. Add the olives and parsley, toss and plate.

NY STRIP STEAK

INGREDIENTS
**2 NY strip steaks, 18 oz. each (yields
enough for 4 – 6 people)
Olive Oil, Sea Salt & Pepper**

TO PREP
Trim off any excess fat from the steak and dry well
using paper towels.

METHOD
1. Get the grill HOT.
2. Coat steaks evenly with Olive Oil, Sea Salt & Pepper.
3. Grill about 5 minutes on each side or until cooked to
your liking.
4. Allow the meat to rest for 10 minutes before slicing.
5. Serve along with your favorite grilled vegetables from
the previous pages and finish the sliced steak with a
drizzle of good extra virgin Olive Oil.

TIPS
* Cover the grill while cooking the thicker cuts of beef.
* Resting the meat allows the juices to distribute. Cutting
into the meat too early will drain the steak of its natural
juices and it will become dry.
* Other cuts, such as hanger, skirt, rib eye, flank, T-bone
and tenderloin, can all be prepared using this same
method.
* Grilled red or sweet onions are an exceptional accompaniment to any grilled steak.

Nothing beats grilling in the summertime…

*except a perfectly ripe heirloom tomato. Large dice a tomato.
Toss in a bowl with fresh basil and extra virgin Olive Oil,
Sea Salt & Pepper. Serve alongside the steak. Yummm!*

*My other favorite way to enjoy steak is with a simple
arugula salad. In a bowl, toss baby arugula with a splash
of balsamic vinegar and extra virgin Olive Oil, Sea Salt &
Pepper. Finish with shaved parmigiano cheese.
Quick and easy!*

LAMB

INGREDIENTS
**4 lamb loin chops (serves 2)
Olive Oil, Sea Salt & Pepper**

TO PREP
Trim off any excess fat from the lamb and dry well
using paper towels.

METHOD
1. Get the grill HOT.
2. Coat lamb evenly with Olive Oil, Sea Salt & Pepper.
3. Grill about 5 – 7 minutes on each side with the grill
covered or until cooked to your liking.
4. Allow the meat to rest for 5 – 10 minutes before
serving.
5. Serve along with your favorite grilled vegetables from
the previous pages and finish the grilled lamb with a
drizzle of good extra virgin Olive Oil.

TIPS
* Resting the meat allows the juices to distribute. Cutting
into the meat too early will drain the lamb of its natural
juices and it will become dry.
* Other cuts, such as rack of lamb, can be prepared using
this same method.
* After cooking, allow the meat to rest on some sprigs of
fresh mint for additional flavor.
* If grilling a rack of lamb, grill on the edge of the grill
with the bones hanging off of the grill. This will keep
them from burning and breaking.
* Grilled lamb goes great with Ratatouille (page 53) or a
Greek salad (page 74), both classic combinations.

CHICKEN

INGREDIENTS

Use any cut, and any amount of chicken: thighs, legs, wings or breasts, skin on Olive Oil, Sea Salt & Pepper

TO PREP

Trim any excess fat to the shape of the chicken pieces.

METHOD

1. Get the grill HOT to heat the grates, then lower to medium heat for cooking.
2. Coat chicken evenly in a bowl with Olive Oil, Sea Salt & Pepper.
3. Grill the chicken on each side on medium heat with the cover closed for 10 – 15 minutes per side or cooked until there is no pink inside. (Chicken breasts typically take 10 – 15 minutes, while dark meat with the bone in takes 20 – 30 minutes total.)
4. Allow the meat to rest for 10 minutes before serving.
5. Serve along with your favorite grilled vegetables from the previous pages and finish the grilled chicken with a drizzle of good extra virgin Olive Oil.

TIPS

* Resting the meat allows the juices to distribute. Cutting into the meat too early will drain the chicken of its natural juices and it will become dry.

* If the meat is burning on the outside, but not cooked on the inside, either lower the heat and close the top of the grill or place the chicken on a sheet pan and finish cooking in a 375 degree oven.

* After grilling you can toss the chicken in the barbeque sauce of your choice. Enjoy as is, or put back on the grill for additional color. Barbeque sauce contains sugar, so if you grill chicken from a raw state covered in barbeque sauce, it will burn on the outside and still be raw on the inside. Better to cook the chicken first and then add the sauce.

GRILLED CHICKEN THIGHS WITH GARLIC-CILANTRO OIL

SERVES 4

INGREDIENTS

**8 chicken thighs, skinless, boneless and grilled as explained in previous recipe
1 cup (packed) cilantro leaves, washed and dried
2 cloves garlic
½ cup extra virgin Olive Oil
½ teaspoon Sea Salt**

Grill chicken as explained in previous recipe. Puree cilantro, garlic, oil and salt in a blender. Brush over grilled chicken and serve.

* Excellent with a summer tomato salad (page 137) or coleslaw (page 143).

PORK

INGREDIENTS
1 pork tenderloin
Olive Oil, Sea Salt & Pepper

TO PREP
Trim off any excess fat from the pork and dry well using paper towels.

METHOD
1. Get the grill HOT.
2. Coat pork evenly with Olive Oil, Sea Salt & Pepper.
3. Grill on medium-high heat with the cover closed for about 10 minutes on each side or until cooked to your liking.
4. Allow the meat to rest for 10 minutes before slicing.
5. Serve along with your favorite grilled vegetables from the previous pages and finish the pork with a drizzle of good extra virgin Olive Oil.

TIPS
* Resting the meat allows the juices to distribute. Cutting into the meat too early will drain the pork of its natural juices and it will become dry.
* Other cuts, such as pork chops, can be prepared using this same method.

PORK WITH PEACH & ARUGULA SALAD

SERVES 2

INGREDIENTS
1 pork tenderloin (about 14 ounces), grilled as explained in previous recipe
1 peach, cut into wedges
2 cups arugula
2 teaspoons balsamic vinegar
1 tablespoon extra virgin Olive Oil
Sea Salt & Pepper

Grill pork as shown above. While the meat is resting, cut the peaches and put them in a bowl. Drizzle the peaches lightly with extra virgin Olive Oil and season lightly with Sea Salt. Grill for about 1 minute per side. Place the arugula in a bowl and dress with Olive Oil and balsamic vinegar and season with Sea Salt & Pepper. Toss and serve with grilled peaches and sliced pork.

BLANCH

Blanching is a cooking term that describes a process of food preparation where the food, in this case a vegetable, is plunged into boiling water, removed after a brief interval and finally plunged into ice water (shocked) to stop the cooking process.

Blanching enhances the color of some (particularly green) vegetables by releasing gases trapped in the food that obscure the greenness of the chlorophyll. Since blanching is done quickly, the heat does not have time to break down chlorophyll, which also enhances the color.

BLANCHING requires a large pot, a bowl, coarse Sea Salt, ice and a slotted spoon or spider.

This method is always the same and is repeated on each page. The only difference is the cooking time. This will vary depending not only on the vegetable but also on the size and thickness of whatever it is you are plunging into the water. When prepping your vegetables, try to keep everything the same size. This will ensure even cooking. If you are not sure about doneness, remove one piece from the water, shock it and taste it. After repeating this method over and over, you will become more comfortable judging the timing. The same blanching water can be used to cook every vegetable mentioned in this section. If you have, for example, green beans, broccoli and carrots to blanch, you can cook them one after the other using the same pot of boiling salted water.

After blanching, you can serve and eat as is, drizzle with extra virgin Olive Oil, Sea Salt & Pepper, reheat in a sauté pan with Olive Oil over medium heat or in the oven at 350 for 1 – 2 minutes (or until warmed through) or store in the fridge for later use.

Blanched vegetables are best eaten the same day they are cooked.

BLANCH NOTES

* Any addition of an acid (tomato, citrus, vinegar, etc.) to the blanching water or to a green vegetable after blanching will result in discoloration of the vegetable.

* Do not crowd the pot! If you need to blanch a lot of vegetables, do it in small batches.

* Do not cover the pot after you add the vegetables. To get the most vibrant colors, keep the top off.

* The goal in blanching is to keep the vegetables green, to brighten the color and to maintain as many of the nutrients as possible. Over-cooking will result in the loss of these benefits.

GREEN BEANS

INGREDIENTS

1 lb. green beans or haricot verts
Sea Salt

TO PREP

Cut or break off the bottom part of the bean (the end that was attached to the plant). Leave the tips on.

METHOD

1. Heat a large pot filled with water on high.
2. Salt the water so that it tastes like the sea.
3. Have the ice water set up in a separate bowl.
4. When the water has reached a hard boil, drop the prepped green beans into the water for 60 – 90 seconds or until they are cooked to your liking.
5. Remove with a slotted spoon or spider and shock in ice water for 1 – 2 minutes.
6. Strain and dry.

TIP

* Green beans will keep up to 3 days. I like to either reheat green beans to serve as a side dish or keep them cold and add them to a salad.

ROMAINE SALAD WITH RED WINE VINAIGRETTE

SERVES 2

INGREDIENTS

1 cup green beans, blanched as explained in previous recipe
1 15-oz. can garbanzo beans, drained, rinsed and dried
15 cherry tomatoes, halved
1 cup cucumber, preferably English, peeled, seeded and diced
1 large head romaine lettuce, cut into half inch strips
½ cup small feta cheese cubes
Sea Salt & Pepper to taste
Basic Red Wine Vinaigrette, as needed (page 178)

Preheat the oven to 350 degrees. In a small bowl toss the garbanzo beans with 1 tablespoon of extra virgin Olive Oil and a little Sea Salt. Toast them on a sheet pan in the oven for 20 minutes, then remove them from the oven and allow to cool. Prepare the vinaigrette on page 178. In a bowl combine the tomatoes, cucumber, romaine, green beans, garbanzo beans and feta. Drizzle dressing over top and toss gently to combine. Season again with Sea Salt & Pepper and serve.

GREEN BEANS WITH ROASTED RED ONION & TOASTED WALNUTS

SERVES 6 AS A SIDE DISH

INGREDIENTS

1 lb. green beans, blanched as explained on page 159
1 medium red onion, sliced
½ cup walnuts, halved
Extra virgin Olive Oil, Sea Salt & Pepper

Preheat the oven to 375 degrees. Toss sliced onions in a bowl with Olive Oil, Sea Salt & Pepper and place on a sheet pan. Roast in the oven for 8 – 10 minutes or until slightly browned. Place the walnuts on a separate sheet pan and drizzle with about a teaspoon of Olive Oil, toss to coat. Toast in a 375 degree oven for 5 – 8 minutes. Remove from the oven and allow to cool. Drizzle 1 – 2 tablespoons of extra virgin Olive Oil over green beans and season with Sea Salt & Pepper as needed. Top with onions and walnuts.

* This is an excellent Thanksgiving side dish and a healthier alternative to the typical green bean casserole.

RED POTATO & HARICOTS VERTS SALAD

SERVES 10

INGREDIENTS

2 lbs. small red potatoes, quartered
8 oz. haricots verts, blanched as explained on page 159 and cut in half on the bias
3 eggs, hard boiled, peeled and large diced (page 68)
½ cup kalamata olives, pitted and halved
1 tablespoon fresh tarragon, chopped
½ cup Mustard Vinaigrette (page 178)
2 tablespoons extra virgin Olive Oil
Sea Salt & Pepper, as needed

Cut the potatoes into quarters and place in a pot with enough water to cover them. Add a teaspoon of Sea Salt and cook over medium heat until they can be pierced easily with a knife. Drain and set aside.
Combine potatoes, egg, olives and haricots verts with the vinaigrette and tarragon. Drizzle with extra virgin Olive Oil and season with Sea Salt & Pepper. This works great as a summer side dish for a picnic or barbeque.

ASPARAGUS

INGREDIENTS
**1 lb. asparagus
Sea Salt**

TO PREP
Cut 2 – 3 inches off the bottom of the asparagus. There is typically a natural breaking point between the top two-thirds of the asparagus and the woody bottom.

METHOD
1. Heat a large pot filled with water on high.
2. Salt the water so that it tastes like the sea.
3. Have your ice water set up in a separate bowl.
4. When the water has reached a hard boil, drop the prepped asparagus into the water for about 2 minutes. The cooking time could be more or less, depending on the thickness of the asparagus.
5. Remove the asparagus with tongs or a spider and shock in ice water for 1 – 2 minutes.
6. Strain and dry.
7. Serve the asparagus as a side dish or use the suggestions below.

TIP
* Asparagus can be pencil thin to thumb thick. Your cooking time will vary depending on the size. When the asparagus is thick I like to peel it before blanching. It is not necessary, but makes for a beautiful presentation.

ASPARAGUS WITH SMOKED SALMON & FRISEE SALAD

SERVES 4

INGREDIENTS
**1 lb. asparagus, woody ends removed, peeled and blanched as explained in previous recipe
8 oz. smoked salmon
2 cups frisee
4 tablespoons Mustard Vinaigrette (page 178)**

Divide asparagus, smoked salmon and frisee onto 4 plates. Spoon one tablespoon of vinaigrette onto each plate and serve.

Another option: add a poached egg to the dish above
**4 eggs
1 tablespoon cider vinegar
4 mason jar rings (optional)**

To poach an egg, fill a saucepan with 2 inches of water and bring to a boil. Lower the heat to a very light simmer and add one tablespoon of cider vinegar to the water (the vinegar helps the egg whites congeal more easily). If you have mason jar rings, place 4 of them in the bottom of the pan. Crack each egg individually into separate small cups or ramekins. Then, gently drop each egg into the water over the mason jar ring and let settle into the ring. With a spoon, nudge the egg whites closer to their yolks. This will help the egg whites hold together. If you don't have rings, don't worry. Just add one egg at a time, allowing each one to congeal before you add the next. Turn off the heat, cover and let sit for 3 minutes, until the egg whites are cooked. Lift eggs out of the pan with a slotted spoon. Great for brunch!

HOW TO BLANCH:
BROCCOLI

INGREDIENTS
1 lb. broccoli
Sea Salt

TO PREP
Using a paring knife, first cut the florets off
the top of the broccoli and then cut into smaller
uniform pieces. Remove the tough outer skin
from the stalk and slice the stalk crosswise into
small disks.

METHOD
1. Heat a large pot filled with water on high.
2. Add enough salt so that it tastes like the sea.
3. Have the ice water set up in a bowl.
4. When the water has reached a hard boil,
drop the prepped broccoli into the water for
2 – 3 minutes.
5. Remove with a slotted spoon or spider and
shock in ice water for 1 minute.
6. Strain and dry.

Broccoli is best used within 3 days of blanching.
Once broccoli is cooked, its shelf life shortens
dramatically. If you smell something foul in your
refrigerator, it is probably the broccoli!

ORECCHIETTE WITH BROCCOLI

SERVES 6

INGREDIENTS

2 lbs. broccoli, blanched as explained on previous page
2 teaspoons garlic, minced
1 lb. orecchiette pasta (or penne)
¼ cup parmesan cheese, grated
Olive Oil, Sea Salt & Pepper
Red chili flakes if desired

Rough chop the blanched broccoli. Using a large sauté pan, over medium high heat, warm ½ cup of extra virgin Olive Oil and minced garlic. Add the broccoli and cook for 2 – 3 minutes. Season with Sea Salt & Pepper (if needed). Cook the pasta in salted water, strain and add to the broccoli. Finish with grated parmesan cheese and extra virgin Olive Oil. Add a pinch of red chili flakes if desired.

I first had this dish in Rome when I was 15. My family made it for dinner every night for 2 weeks straight when we returned home. We could not get enough! It continues to be a family favorite.

CARROTS

INGREDIENTS

1 lb. baby carrots
Sea Salt

TO PREP

Peel carrots and cut off tops and bottom tails. Leave whole if small and cut larger carrots in half or into quarters, depending on thickness, to get them as uniform in size as possible.

METHOD

1. Heat a large pot filled with water on high.
2. Add enough salt to the water so that it tastes like the sea.
3. Have the ice water set up in a bowl.
4. When the water has reached a hard boil, drop the prepped carrots into the water for 60 – 90 seconds.
5. Remove with a slotted spoon or spider and shock in ice water for 1 minute.
6. Strain and dry.

TIPS

* To check for doneness, remove one carrot, shock it and eat it. The carrots should not be completely soft, but should have a bite and a slight crunch.
* Serving suggestion: In a bowl, toss the blanched carrots with chopped cilantro and extra virgin Olive Oil and season with Sea Salt & Pepper. Serve with sautéed halibut (page 67) and sautéed spinach (page 55).

MARINATED CARROTS

SERVES 8 – 10 AS A SIDE DISH

INGREDIENTS

2 lbs. carrots, blanched as explained in previous recipe
3 cloves garlic, peeled and smashed
3 sprigs fresh oregano
¼ cup extra virgin Olive Oil
Sea Salt & Pepper to taste

Marinate carrots in extra virgin Olive Oil, Sea Salt, fresh oregano and two cloves of garlic overnight. These carrots are a nice addition to an antipasto display. Serve at room temperature.

SNAP PEAS

INGREDIENTS
1 lb. snap peas or snow peas
Sea Salt

TO PREP
Cut off tops and remove the string on the inside of
each snap pea.

METHOD
1. Heat a large pot filled with water.
2. Add enough salt so that it tastes like the sea.
3. Have your ice water set up in a bowl.
4. When the water has reached a hard boil, drop the
snap peas into the water for 20 – 30 seconds.
5. Remove with a slotted spoon or spider and shock in
ice water for 1 minute.
6. Strain and dry.

TIPS
* Snap peas are best blanched and eaten the same day.
They are perfect for snacking but will only keep for 24
hours. After a day, they begin to brown.
* Snap peas and asparagus are excellent as a snack with
hummus or paired with any fish.

PEAS

INGREDIENTS

8 oz. fresh peas
Sea Salt

TO PREP

Often you can find fresh English peas in the pod in the spring at the farmer's market. If you are able to find them sold this way, simply use your thumbs to open the pea pod. Turn the pod inside out and push the peas out into a bowl. Discard the pod. Fresh peas are more typically sold already out of the pod and packaged in the produce section of the grocery store. The prep work is already done!

METHOD

1. Heat a large pot filled with water on high.
2. Add enough salt to the water so that it tastes like the sea.
3. Have the ice water set up in a separate bowl.
4. When the water has reached a hard boil, drop the peas into the water for 30 – 60 seconds.
5. Remove with a slotted spoon or spider and shock in ice water for 1 minute.
6. Strain and dry.

ORECCHIETTE WITH MUSHROOMS, PEAS & PARMESAN

SERVES 5

INGREDIENTS

1 lb. orecchiette pasta, cooked in salted water
1 medium sweet onion, sliced
1 teaspoon garlic, minced
12 oz. crimini mushrooms (or baby bella), sliced
1 teaspoon chopped fresh thyme
Extra virgin Olive Oil, Sea Salt & Pepper as needed
1 cup peas, blanched as explained in previous recipe
½ cup parmesan cheese, grated

Bring a large pot of salted water to a boil and cook the pasta as instructed until done and strain. Heat a large sauté pan on high. Sauté sliced onion in 3 tablespoons of Olive Oil for 3 minutes. Add minced garlic, mushrooms and thyme. Season with Sea Salt & Pepper and cook for 1 – 2 minutes. Add cooked pasta and then toss with peas and parmesan cheese. Drizzle with good extra virgin Olive Oil. This is one of my daughter's favorites!

CRUDITÉS

INGREDIENTS

2 lbs. baby carrots, blanched as explained on page 167 (white or yellow carrots if possible)

½ lb. snap peas, blanched as explained on page 169

½ lb. snow peas, blanched as explained on page 169

1 bunch asparagus, blanched as explained on page 162

½ lb. haricot verts, blanched as explained on page 159

1 – 2 endive

1 jicama

1 cucumber, cut into sticks

1 bunch breakfast radishes, cut in half (regular radishes are fine if the breakfast variety is not available)

2 cups hummus or dip of choice

Store the blanched carrots, snap peas, snow peas and haricot verts in the refrigerator until ready to use. Cut the bottom off the endive and break apart into individual leaves. Store in cold ice water until ready to display. Cut the top and bottom off of the jicama. Remove the outer skin with a knife and cut into ½ inch slices then cut again into ½ inch sticks. Store in cold water in the refrigerator until ready to use.

To serve, display all of the vegetables on one large platter or individually along with the hummus or dip in a separate bowl.

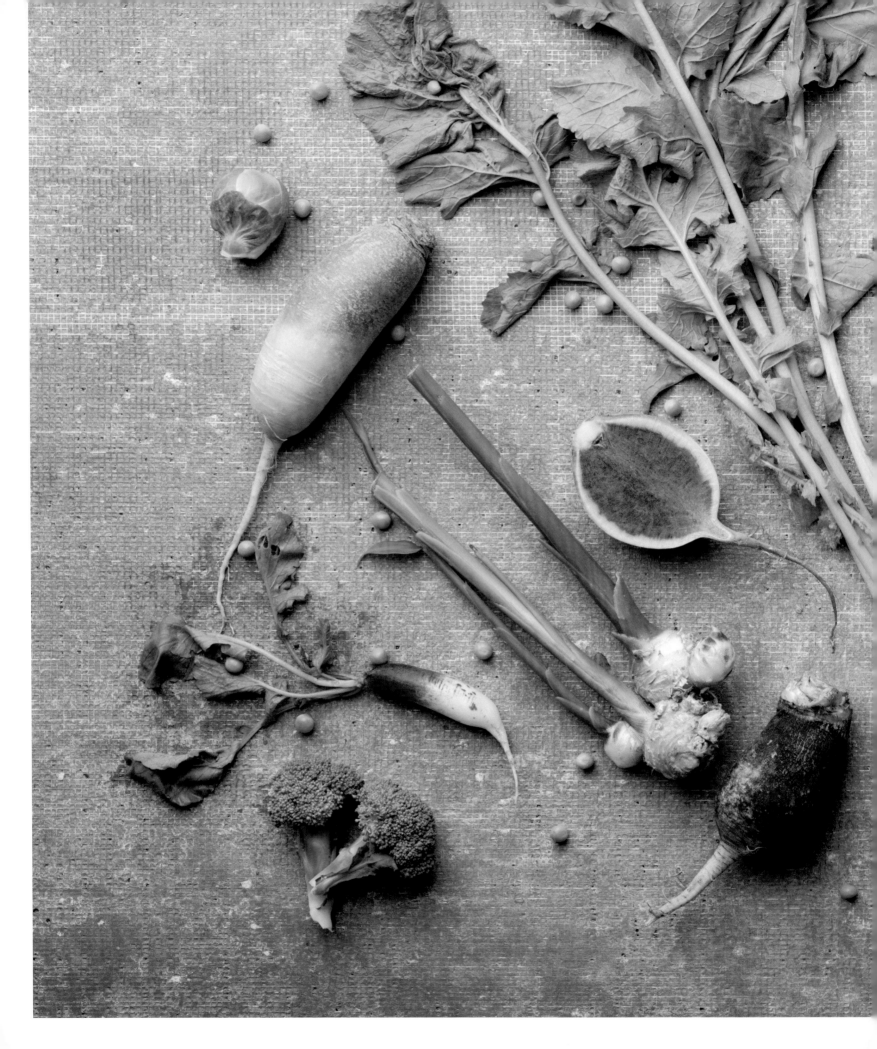

VINAIGRETTES

VINAIGRETTE is a mixture of oil and vinegar. Typical ratios are 3- to- 1: 3 parts oil, 1 part vinegar (or acid). If you want to liberally drizzle oil and vinegar over your salad, keep those ratios in mind. If you are a salad lover, as I am, make a large batch of vinaigrette and store it in a plastic squeeze bottle in the refrigerator to use conveniently throughout the month. You will appreciate the quality of your homemade vinaigrette compared with the store-bought variety. Vinaigrette variations are described on the following pages. The type you choose can be determined by personal ingredient preference or simply by what you have available in your kitchen cabinet. Bigger batches are easier to make in a blender and smaller individual portions are better whisked in a bowl.

DIRECTIONS FOR USING A BLENDER:
Put all ingredients except the oil in the blender. While blending, slowly add the oil until all ingredients are incorporated.

DIRECTIONS FOR USING A BOWL:
If you do not have a blender, or are making smaller portions, use a large bowl and a whisk. In the same way as above, combine all ingredients except the oil. Slowly incorporate the oil while constantly whisking until the ingredients are completely emulsified.
When dressing your greens, use just enough to coat them. You do not want them drowning in vinaigrette. Remember, you can always add, but you cannot take away. Add just a little at a time until your salad is dressed to your liking.

VINAIGRETTES WHISKED IN A BOWL

BASIC LEMON VINAIGRETTE
Ingredients:
2 tablespoons fresh lemon juice
¼ cup extra virgin Olive Oil
Sea Salt & Pepper to taste

BASIC RED WINE VINAIGRETTE
Ingredients:
2 tablespoons red wine vinegar
6 tablespoons extra virgin Olive Oil
Sea Salt & Pepper

BASIC BALSAMIC VINAIGRETTE
Ingredients:
1 tablespoon balsamic vinegar
3 tablespoons extra virgin Olive Oil
Sea Salt & Pepper to taste

LEMON-DIJON VINAIGRETTE
Ingredients:
1 teaspoon Dijon mustard
2 tablespoons lemon juice
1 shallot, finely chopped
½ cup extra virgin Olive Oil
Sea Salt & Pepper to taste

MAPLE CIDER VINAIGRETTE
Ingredients:
2 teaspoons pure maple syrup
2 teaspoons apple cider vinegar
1 tablespoon minced shallots
2 teaspoons Dijon mustard
2 tablespoons extra virgin Olive Oil
Sea Salt & Pepper to taste

APPLE CIDER VINAIGRETTE
Ingredients:
2 tablespoons apple cider vinegar
2 teaspoons Dijon mustard
¼ cup extra virgin Olive Oil
2 teaspoons honey
Sea Salt & Pepper to taste

MUSTARD VINAIGRETTE
This is my most versatile vinaigrette. I also use it
as a sauce for salmon, crab cakes, over asparagus
or to dress potato salad.

Ingredients:
2 tablespoons Dijon mustard
1 tablespoon whole grain mustard
2 teaspoons balsamic vinegar
2 teaspoons sherry vinegar
1 tablespoon honey
¼ cup Olive Oil
1 tablespoon orange juice
Sea Salt & Pepper to taste

VINAIGRETTES USING A BLENDER

RED WINE DIJON VINAIGRETTE

Ingredients:

2 tablespoons fresh lemon juice

2 tablespoons red wine vinegar

2 tablespoons Dijon mustard

2 cloves garlic, minced

½ cup extra virgin Olive Oil

½ teaspoon Sea Salt

Freshly ground Pepper, to taste

BALSAMIC VINAIGRETTE

Ingredients:

1 cup balsamic vinegar

2 tablespoons garlic

¼ cup Dijon mustard

3 cups extra virgin Olive Oil

Sea Salt & Pepper to taste

CUCUMBER DRESSING

Ingredients:

1 small cucumber, peeled, seeded and chopped

¼ cup extra virgin Olive Oil

2 tablespoons red wine vinegar

2 tablespoons fresh chives, chopped

2 tablespoons tarragon

2 tablespoons fresh parsley, chopped

1 tablespoon Greek yogurt

2 teaspoon Dijon mustard

1 teaspoon prepared horseradish

$1/8$ teaspoon Sea Salt

GINGER-SOY VINAIGRETTE

I could eat this with a spoon! I was a little hesitant to put it in this book because it does not follow the theme, but I figured what the heck, it is really good!

Ingredients:

3 cloves garlic

2 tablespoons fresh ginger, minced

$1/3$ cup rice vinegar

½ cup soy sauce

3 tablespoons honey

¼ cup sesame oil

½ cup Olive Oil

ROASTED TOMATO VINAIGRETTE

Ingredients:

¼ cup oven roasted tomatoes, as explained on page 104, skins removed

1 teaspoon garlic, minced

3 large basil leaves

3 tablespoons extra virgin Olive Oil

2 tablespoons sherry vinegar

Sea Salt & Pepper to taste

MENU IDEAS FOR ENTERTAINING

Below are groupings of menu ideas for different entertaining scenarios using recipes from *Olive Oil, Sea Salt & Pepper*.

COCKTAIL BUFFET

A cocktail buffet is a perfect option when you are having guests over just for drinks and you do not plan to serve dinner, but instead want to offer lighter foods on which your guests can graze. Below is a menu made from ingredients and foods that will do well sitting out at room temperature.

Charcuterie Display — prosciutto, bresaola and salami (serve with fresh figs if they are in season)

Cheese Display — Typically one of each: cow, goat, sheep and a blue cheese

Cheese Accompaniments — crackers, baguette, honey, nuts, dried cherries and apricots

Olives

Mushroom & Goat Cheese Tart (page 40)

Roasted cauliflower with golden raisins & toasted pine nuts (page 99)

Lentils (page 114)

Couscous with Roasted Asparagus, Fennel & Shitakes (page 101)

Marinated Carrots (page 167)

THANKSGIVING SIDE DISHES

Below are recipes that offer enjoyable options for Thanksgiving side dishes.

Sautéed Brussels Sprout Leaves with Bacon, Corn & Onions (page 39)

Green Beans with Roasted Red Onion & Toasted Walnuts (page 160) (great alternative to green bean casserole)

Butternut Squash with Lentils & Arugula (page 43)

Sautéed Collard Greens with Turnip & Bacon (page 55)

Roasted Butternut Squash & Red Leaf Salad (page 93)

Barley with Fall Vegetables (page 90)

BARBEQUES, PICNICS AND POTLUCKS

Grilled Chicken Thighs with Garlic-Cilantro Oil (page 150)

Barbequed Salmon (page 143)

Red Potato & Haricots Verts Salad (page 160)

Coleslaw (page 143)

Lemon Quinoa with Grilled Asparagus & Olives (page 133)

Mixed grill of scallops & shrimp (page 141)

Grilled vegetable couscous (page 141)

Grilled Corn, Tomato & Basil Salad (page 137)

HORS D'OEUVRES

Grilled Cauliflower with Black Olive
   Vinaigrette (page 138)
Roasted Shitake & Taleggio Crostini
   (page 94)
Bruschetta with oven roasted plum
   tomatoes & ricotta (page 104)
Grilled Zucchini & Goat Cheese Rolls
   (page 132)
Crudités (page 172)

BRUNCH

Asparagus with Smoked Salmon
   & Frisee Salad (page 162)
Sweet potato hash (page 47)
Mushroom & Goat Cheese Tart (page 40)
Fresh fruit, yogurt and granola (purchase
   fruit that is in season)

DINNER BUFFET

Oven Roasted Shrimp with Lemon
   & Basil Orzo (page 116)
Beef Tenderloin with horseradish cream
   (page 123)
Grilled vegetables — asparagus, carrots,
   zucchini, eggplant and peppers
   (pages 129 – 134)
Orecchiette with Broccoli (page 166)
Romaine Salad with Red Wine Vinaigrette
   (page 159)

FAJITA NIGHT

Fajitas (page 48)
Chicken quesadillas with guacamole
   (page 121)
Grilled Corn with Edamame
   & Black Beans (page 137)
Mixed green salad with manchego,
   dried cherry & pecan (page 73)

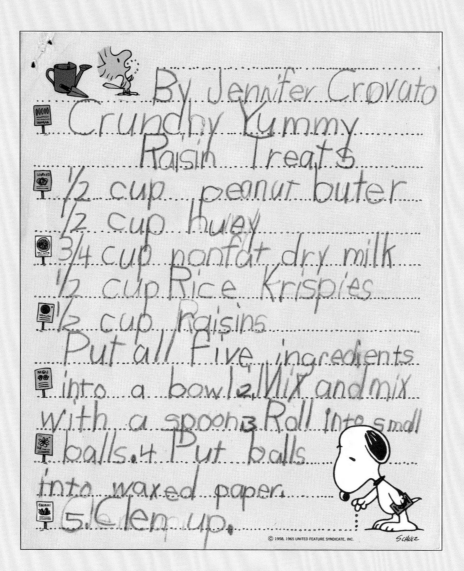

By Jennifer Crovato

Crunchy Yummy
Raisin Treats

½ cup peanut buter
½ cup huey
¾ cup nonfat dry milk
½ cup Rice Krispies
½ cup Raisins

Put all five ingredients
into a bowl 1. 2. Mix and mix
with a spoon 3. Roll into small
balls. 4 Put balls
into waxed paper.
5. 6 Clean up.

Jenn's first recipe, written at age 6 and
sold to a family friend for 25¢!

INDEX

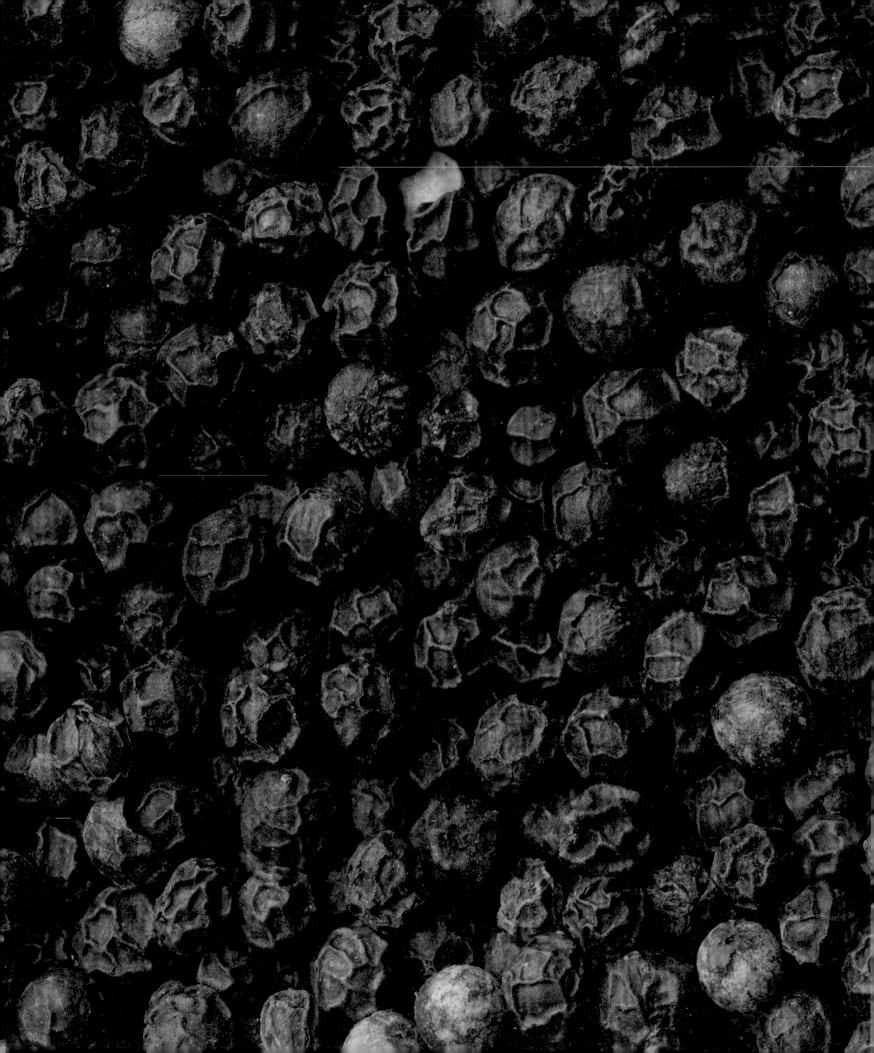